ALSO BY JAMES VAN SWEDEN
(WITH WOLFGANG OEHME AND SUSAN RADEMACHER FREY)

Bold Romantic Gardens

GARDENING WITH
WATER

GARDENING WITH
WATER

JAMES VAN SWEDEN

RANDOM HOUSE · NEW YORK

The photograph on page iii is by Richard Felber; the photographs on pages iv, v, and viii are
by Roger Foley.

This work is published with the understanding that Random House and its author are supply-
ing information but are not attempting to render engineering or other professional services. If
such services are required, the assistance of an appropriate professional should be sought.

Library of Congress Cataloging-in-Publication Data
van Sweden, James.
Gardening with water: how James van Sweden and Wolfgang Oehme build and
plant fountains, swimming pools, lily pools, water edges/James van Sweden.
p. cm.
Includes bibliographical references (p. 199) and index.
ISBN 0-679-42946-8
1. Water in landscape architecture. 2. Water gardens. I. Title.
SB475.8.V35 1994
714—dc20   94-28213

Manufactured in the United States of America on acid-free paper
9 8 7 5 4 3 2
First Edition

DESIGNED BY JOEL AVIROM & JASON SNYDER

To the memory of
Henry Clay Mitchell

A large fish pool or pond, stocked with hardy waterlilies and goldfish and a variety of interesting plants (arrowheads, yellow water irises, thalias, rushes, striped acorus, etc.) in and around the pool here and there is almost labor free.

Much of the charm of such a feature is its freedom from drought and disease. There is endless pleasure to be had from frogs and toads, from dragonflies and damselflies that come unbidden and make the long summer days vibrate with life.

H.C.M.

PREFACE

Water is life itself—the magical element that connects all creation. All God's creatures are irresistibly drawn to the watering hole. Shape-shifter, stone carver, cooler, quencher, cleanser, bringer of messages in bottles, water is the magnet and mirror of life, the ultimate animator of gardens.

It is fitting that James van Sweden and Wolfgang Oehme chose water as the subject of this first book of a new series. Water is the natural partner in the ever-changing dance of vegetative life and death that is the signature of their gardens.

James and Wolfgang bring a generous attitude to crafting this book. They don't keep trade secrets. Confident in their originality and mastery, they want to share design principles and techniques evolved over a partnership of twenty years. Following the tenets of their first book, *Bold Romantic Gardens: The New World Landscapes of Oehme and van Sweden,* James and Wolfgang have produced a volume of great utility and inspiration. Readers will appreciate its clarity of structure and illustrations and enjoy the lyrical writing and photography.

James authors this book, not surprisingly, for his is the principal voice of the partnership. Each garden has its own voice, however. It is the voice of the place itself, made plush and earthy and well seasoned. Leaves whisper and rub together, water sings, winged creatures buzz and trill, dried husks rattle, people respond with delight.

These are gardens of generous spirit, all-embracing and exuberant. At the heart of that spirit is a set of values that can guide each of us in creating our own great gardens. Personal experience is each design's starting point. Ease of care is primarily achieved by wise plant selection. A bold layout that creates mystery, refined construction details, and a planting design based on naturalistic principles all help to stimulate and free the imagination.

Above all, these water gardens "vibrate with life," in the words of the great garden writer Henry Mitchell. Enter them with imagination. Try them on for size. Enlarge your sense of what a garden can be when form and detail provide the framework for liberating sensuality. And, finally, delight in receiving the sensory gift of keen awareness that we can all bring to daily life in the natural world.

— Susan M. Rademacher

David Hockney, Day Pool with Three Blues
(Paper Pool 7), 1978. Pressed colored paper pulp.
72" x 85 ¹/₂". © David Hockney/
Tylar Graphics, Ltd.

ACKNOWLEDGMENTS

First I wish to acknowledge the partnership I have had with Wolfgang Oehme for twenty years. We are very different in temperament and approach to design. Wolfgang comes to landscape architecture from horticulture and I from architecture. We meet in the middle, where I think the total is definitely more than the sum of the parts.

In writing this book I am amazed by the number of encouraging and supportive people I have met. Helen Pratt, my literary agent, shared the vision from the beginning and introduced me to Random House and my editor, Jason Epstein, who has given generous support and many helpful suggestions. Robin Herbst was invaluable as a reader and commentator on the final manuscript. Joel Avirom designed this beautiful book with panache and good humor. Benjamin Zelenko gave sage legal counsel.

Barbara Bolling Woodward accompanied me on many study trips abroad with limitless energy, creative insights, and remarkable breadth of inquiry.

Several of the gardens that follow were designed in successful collaboration with other landscape architects and architects. These include M. Paul Friedberg, Lester Collins, Hugh Newell Jacobsen, and Stephen Carr.

Generous assistance and encouragement were given by H. Marc Cathey, John Brookes, Michael Laurie, Conrad Hamerman, Roberto Burle Marx, Mien Ruys, Shiro Nakane, Tsunekata Naito, Sylvester March, Martha Turner, and Susan Rademacher. Personal thanks go to my mother, Johanna van Sweden, and to my friend and mentor Margaret Holmes.

Wolgang and I recognize the crucial support of our dedicated staff. Charles E. Turner wrote and edited much of the text with me. Project landscape architects who brought many of the projects on the "garden tour" to fruition are Sandra Youssef Clinton, Eric D. Groft, Sheila A. Brady, Lawrence V. Frank, and Nancy Watkins Denig. Jeff Charlesworth produced the beautiful pencil drawings. Research for the "Build" and "Plant" sections was done by Bruce J. Riddell and René M. Albacete. Lisa E. Delplace, H. Paul Davis, and Eileen Emmet gave valuable support. Excellent clerical assistance on the word processor was given by Mai Scannapieco. Marcia Kinder Oresky kept accurate accounts.

Also of great value has been the craftsmanship of James Birks, a master builder in brick and stone, and the assistance of Michael and Audrey Wyatt and Pauline Vollmer.

CONTENTS

INTRODUCTION

Gardening with Water celebrates the universal joy that water brings, especially in the garden setting. Water can play a role in any garden, no matter the budget or the garden's size. Even if the part it plays is a small one, water will magnify the pleasures of your private paradise.

Water plays a crucial role in our designs, so I decided to make it the subject of the first book in a general series of volumes on the subject of garden design. This book gives me the opportunity to share our design secrets and to tell you how we work with water. The book discusses water's many uses and presents designs through plans, sections, construction details, and specifications. A glossary of our favorite plants for water, marsh, wetlands, and on the upland edge explains their nuances and includes USDA zones, type, height, conditions, and characteristics. Throughout I have written an informal text that provides straightforward information while conveying the joys of designing and living with a garden that contains water—regardless of its size or challenges. When we garden with water we can indulge our fantasies.

Throughout history, gardens have evolved most spectacularly wherever water was abundant or could be channeled to flow. In early Egypt and Mesopotamia water was a precarious resource; it had to be husbanded, lured into sophisticated patterns to irrigate vegetable and herb gardens. Over time, the channels used for agriculture evolved into decorative canal systems and ponds containing fish and water plants, such as lotus and papyrus. The notion that paradise could be mirrored here on earth, in the form of a terrestrial oasis, first took root in Egypt and then moved west.

Historically, water has transformed every environment to which it has been introduced, from the desert groves of Egypt to the English pastoral landscapes of the eighteenth century created by British landscape gardener Lancelot "Capability" Brown. You can find the same cross-axial grid used in early Islamic water gardens underpinning the seventeenth-century designs of Versailles and Vaux-le-Vicomte, and in the nineteenth- and twentieth-century American gardens such as the perennial border at Central Park designed by Frederick Law Olmsted and Beatrix Ferrand's design for Dumbarton Oaks.

In my garden, the shallow concave top of a pottery lantern by Marie Woo fills with water and acts as a mirror, reflecting Tulipa 'Red Shine' (lily flowered tulip). The three spheres are by sculptor Grace Knowlton.

Whether introduced out of necessity—for feeding animals or irrigating plants—or for sheer pleasure, water's effect is the same. It expands and enriches the world around it; it cools and makes the air lighter, reflects movement and color, and creates a constant music.

Leave a dish of water outside for a few minutes. When you check back you may find you've attracted a few finches for a drink. The sun and clouds are reflected there; you can even see the wind's rippling fingerprint. It's that easy to start a water garden.

In my own garden I use the concave top of a pottery lantern made by Marie Woo for a birdbath. I wouldn't think of changing the original design of the garden by introducing a constructed water feature. But most gardens benefit from the formal introduction of a pond, a swimming pool, a fountain. Even small suburban backyards will seem larger or have more diversity with a pond or pool or both. The amount of available space and your budget will determine the proper scale of your pond, fountain, or pool. The simplest water forms built from ordinary materials are often the most beautiful. Gardening with water is a rewarding challenge on every scale, and the same design principles apply to each one.

Using This Book

In Part I, "Inspirations," I draw practical examples of the proper use of water from fine works by my peers in the United States and abroad. I have included garden designers with a sympathetic approach from the United States, such as Robert Zion and Thomas Church. Those from abroad include Roberto Burle Marx in Brazil, John Brookes in England, and Mien Ruys in the Netherlands. Landmarks such as Buckingham Fountain on the Chicago lakefront, the lake at Shugaku-in Detached Palace in Kyoto, Japan, and the Great Fountain at the Herrenhäuser in Hanover, Germany, put my work in historical context.

I believe every garden benefits from the decorative use of water, regardless of budget or size. To prove this thesis, in Part II, "Design," I have arranged a "tour" of our water designs from my own nine-inch concave pottery lantern top, which holds just a half-inch of water after a rain and brings birds and the reflection of sky into the foreground of my small city garden, to Rock Rim Ponds, a 254-acre property in Pound Ridge, New York, where I practice gardening with water on the broad scale of the residential community. Each design unfolds through text, photographs, and drawings. A short introductory essay describes the geographical and vernacular context, the inherent problems and opportunities, and our design response. A series of plans illustrates the landscape design of the water feature and the planting design. In the case of a garden that contains several bodies of water, I show how they relate in a master plan. And whenever topography is important, I have drawn a section through the landscape showing elevations of water elements and topographic changes in the garden.

In Part III, "Build," and Part IV, "Plant," I discuss the technical aspects of putting our water gardens together. Part III contains construction details in photographs and drawings, cross-referenced wherever possible to a specific design on the garden tour in Part II. I have also used this technique in listing our favorite water plants by showing each, where possible, cross-referenced to photographs and drawings in a water-garden context.

I always refer to plants by their botanical names, with common names given in parentheses if the plant is not included in the glossary. When a plant is referred to as a general category, the abbreviation *spp.* is used instead of the specific species. This should ensure accuracy, since common names vary widely.

In Part V, "Care," I discuss in detail the maintenance of a water design, including how to achieve the biological balance necessary for a clear lily pool, and the proper method of cleaning the filter weekly and removing debris.

In Part VI, "Rules and Regulations," I simply remind you to check the local laws that pertain to water design in your area. Depth, size, and setback are just a few of the elements of design that the law may determine. It is very important for you to be familiar with your local building codes and obtain the required permits before implementing your own water design. Since it contains such detailed information, Wolfgang and I hope this book will be a source of study and inspiration to you for many years to come.

FOLLOWING PAGE: A basin of water or tsukubai honors the ritual of purification in the Japanese garden. The bamboo on top supports the ladle while the water pours from the bamboo shishi odoshi.

PART I

INSPIRATIONS

GARDENING WITH WATER

For me, growing up meant having fun with water in all its forms. Like most kids, I played in the bathtub with my toy boats and ran through the sprinkler over wet lawns on hot days. I spent my childhood summers at Lake Michigan—lying on the golden sand beaches, riding waves in the fresh water, gliding along in an old rowboat, or water-skiing behind my uncle's Chris-Craft. I also loved exploring the edges of streams and ponds in our neighborhood.

When I was six I had my own fishpond. I caught tadpoles, frogs, and fish for the pond and had fun watching the tadpoles turn into frogs. I netted mosquito larvae from water drums, dug up worms, and collected caterpillars from rosebushes to feed the fish. The pond taught me my first practical lessons in designing with water, including the special needs of aquatic life and plants. It seemed I was always on my hands and knees looking into the water.

In the winter we went to Florida, where I enjoyed the pure powder-white beaches of the Gulf of Mexico and fished on the Caloosahatchee River among the mangrove islands. Florida was rich in examples of "designed" water—from the Cypress Gardens, with its Spanish moss suspended above ponds whose mirror-smooth surfaces reflected girls in crinoline petticoats, to Tarpon Springs, where we used to take rides in glass-bottomed boats. I particularly used to love watching the water in the foun-

Bubbling higoi koi *add life, color, and motion to this water-garden scene.*
ROGER FOLEY PHOTOGRAPH

tains change color after dark. How could I visit Florida and not be influenced by water in all of its decorative forms?

Chicago was the first big city I ever saw. While I was there I visited Buckingham Fountain, the biggest lighted fountain in the world, inspired by the Neptune Fountain at Versailles. The deafening sound of the rushing water, the shifting reflections, and the spectacle of colored lights after nightfall transported me. Talk about a fantasy! The designer's vision matched the city's scale and exuberance. Buckingham Fountain still provides the fireworks for summer evenings on the Chicago waterfront.

One of my first inspirations occurred while I was a student at the University of Michigan at Ann Arbor. There I first heard of Frank Lloyd Wright and the house he called Falling Water, located at Bear Run, Pennsylvania. I studied Falling Water's design and began to understand the connection between architecture and landscape. Wright succeeded by closely tying the house to its rugged setting. Falling Water inspired me to look at setting as well as structure. Water clearly was the star of this show.

BELOW: Buckingham Fountain on the Chicago waterfront, designed by Edward Bennett, matches the city's scale and exuberance.
OPPOSITE: Falling Water at Bear Run, Pennsylvania, designed by Frank Lloyd Wright, beautifully connects architecture to landscape. Water is the essence of this landmark design.
HAROLD CORSINI PHOTOGRAPH

TOP: *The nineteenth-century Bethesda Fountain in New York City's Central Park, designed by Frederick Law Olmsted, is shown here with its popular "lake" and terrace in full use.*
Thomas Sears Collection, Smithsonian Institution Archives of American Gardens, Washington, D.C.

ABOVE: *New York City's Paley Park, designed by Zion & Breen Associates, features a "water wall" that masks city noise and brings the cooling effect of water into this urban lunch scene.*

OPPOSITE: *In a recent design, Mien Ruys used recycled plastic to create a "stepping-stone" bridge which seems to hover over the water, perfectly matching this artificial material to the natural garden around it.*

I loved Falling Water's setting so much that I shifted the emphasis of my architectural studies from the building to the landscape. I decided that further travel would be a great source of inspiration for me; I longed to see the world.

I began by exploring New York City. I was captivated by Frederick Law Olmsted's design for Central Park, with its great mall, which had the Bethesda Fountain at its north end, and the lake dotted with rowboats and canoes. For a small-town boy like me, the park embodied nineteenth-century urban splendor.

Later I traveled to Europe, where I discovered that for me the best way to grasp the many facets of urban design was to study at the world's most densely populated urban center, the Netherlands. Water is an obsession among the Dutch. I soon realized that there was no better place than Holland to enjoy and study all of its possible design forms. Water is omnipresent in Holland, from the placid canals flanked by fields of grazing cows to the medieval water pumps that grace lovely town squares.

In Holland I discovered the designs of the great Dutch landscape architect Mien Ruys, whose work has inspired me ever since. Her use of water in natural landscapes is exemplary, and after seventy years of experimentation, she has refined both the detail and proportion of her work. Recently I visited Ruys's nursery, now a National Trust property, which is a record of her development as a designer, beginning with the lily pool she designed when she was seventeen. One of her most recent designs is a marsh garden, which she finished the year before I visited. The proportions and details of these gardens are exquisite.

LEFT: Beth Chatto has created a massive bog planting at her Unusual Plants Nursery in Essex. Shown here on an August afternoon is an example of her genius: plants of various textures, colors, and sizes are combined to transform an ordinary drainage ditch into a series of beautifully landscaped ponds.

RIGHT: The cruciform shape of this lily pool, designed by John Brookes, adds serenity and contrast to the exuberant plantings in and around it. The water surface rises almost to the top, and delicate jets of arching water from each corner of the crossing create a splash at the center.

I went to England next. The English landscape has always been a source of creative replenishment for me. I particularly love the grand scale of the esplanade on both sides of the Thames at Westminster. At Blenheim and Stowe I discovered the subtle impact of designing with water on a vast scale and the romantic effect of reflected water. The rush of water down the cascade at Chatsworth is overwhelming. These works free the imagination.

Contemporary British designers Beth Chatto and John Brookes have taught me a great deal about plant design as it relates to the water's edge and about the importance of "transitioning" plants from immersion level to marshland and upland. Chatto's "damp" garden was created by damming up a spring-fed ditch to form a series of calm pools reflecting a lush garden of water-loving plants. Brookes is a noted garden writer and designer. He has created many beautiful gardens and shares his secrets generously in his books. Both have influenced my designs of paving and edging materials, sculpture, planting, and pool forms.

Garden shows in Germany have influenced my designs in many ways. They exhibit a range of ideas, including interesting play areas for children that feature "mud streams" for making mud pies, and gigantic fountains with lights and music in vast reflecting pools edged with café terraces.

As a student touring Germany I was amazed by the Great Fountain in the garden of the Herrenhausen, near Hanover. This early eighteenth-century garden, with its fountains designed by M. Charbonnier, was inspired by French garden traditions and the House of Orange. The garden is divided by crossed paths with the great fountain at the center. The placement of planting, paths, and water provides lessons in good proportion. The Great Fountain illustrates how water focuses a garden space.

TOP LEFT: *Karl Foerster's garden in Potsdam features a lily pool in a rectangular garden space. The pool reflects layered plants of contrasting texture, shape, and leaf size.*
LEFT: *La Serre de la Madone, in Menton, planned by Lawrence Johnson, is shown here as a romantic "ruin" about to be restored. It is a perfect marriage of planting, sculpture, and water.*
OPPOSITE TOP: *The Fountain Stravinsky in Paris, by Jean Tinguely and Niki de Saint-Phalle, is a carnival of reflection, color, motion, and sound. Its special magnetism is irresistible on this warm summer afternoon.*
OPPOSITE BOTTOM: *Water is the star of the show at Planten un Blomen in Hamburg, designed by Karl Plomin in 1953. Terraced pools on a grand scale reflect lush plantings and add seemingly endless depth to the garden scene.*
WOLFGANG OEHME PHOTOGRAPH

Japan was a shock. I realized I was looking into the next century. The throngs of people, the glitter, the speeding bullet trains, and Japanese infatuation with technology are stunning. In this cosmopolitan bustle, where would I find gardens, let alone water?

The answer lay in a few exquisite public oases in Tokyo and in the many temple gardens of Kyoto. Japanese gardens are designed to be full of mystery; they lure you through the smallest entrance garden to the door of a restaurant or through the three garden spaces at the great garden of Shugaku-in Detached Palace. Every space is layered and almost every design includes water along its path. Often the illusion of water is created by a visual "dry stream," in which a meandering line of rocks, river stones, and gravel leads the eye into and through the garden.

Japanese gardens inspired me to study the meaning of each element in a garden's design, particularly water. The Japanese appreciate scale; they will, for example, create a lily pool as large as possible in proportion to its garden space. Before my visits to Japan I designed pools that were too small for their environments. I learned from Japanese gardens that such pools should be as large as the

space allows. It is important that water features not look skimpy; they should be more than a curious detail without relevance to the total design. Water must be used as a dramatic element, pulling in the sky's mutable light, creating a dynamic foil to plantings and rocks, and imparting the illusion of an enlarged garden space. After seeing exquisitely proportioned Japanese pools surrounded by the simplest details of buildings, stones, and plants, my approach to design would never be the same.

OPPOSITE TOP: *A collection of stone garden ornaments adorn the corner of a tiny garden shop in the suburbs of Kyoto.*
OPPOSITE BOTTOM & TOP: *A stream through the moss gardens of Hakone Museum of Art in Hakone Park reflects the vivid colors of Acer palmatum (Japanese maple) in October. Water rushes over smooth white river stones carefully laid on the stream bottom.*
LEFT: *A serpentine pattern of lawn at water's edge, decorative timber poles, and welcoming path inspire strolling in the garden at the Sento Palace in Kyoto. Visitors delight in the changing panorama as they walk along the shore of the lake.*
OVERLEAF: *A beautifully proportioned lily pool at the entrance foyer of a private home in Tokyo enlivens the composition of architecture, terrace, and soft landscape frame.*

The water designs of Roberto Burle Marx in Brazil inspire with their size and drama, whether they reflect the mountains or act as a foil for the large leaves of plants such as *Monstera deliciosa* (split-leaf philodendron). On hot, tropical winter days, the cooling presence of water is essential, and Burle Marx always seems to include it in his designs.

Burle Marx's most dramatic examples of integrating water with architecture are found in Brasília, where the Department of State literally stands in a pool of water and the Ministry of Justice has immense weirs of cascading water off the building façade itself. Burle Marx's designs feature islands of plants and often sculpture in large pools. There is nothing timid about how he uses water or embellishes his designs with the overblown lushness of his tropical palette: *Pleurospa arborescens* (arum spp.), *Thalia geniculata* (water canna), and *Victoria regia* (royal water lily). The lily pool with its water "wall" in Burle Marx's own garden is a beautiful mosaic of found objects constructed as a sculptural wall with jets of water spouting from strategic places. It contrasts with the large pool's placid surface, brimming with water plants.

LEFT: Water cascades off immense weirs that are part of the façade of the Ministry of Justice Building in Brasília.
OPPOSITE TOP: A wall made of old, granite building stones creates a backdrop for a large lily pool in the garden of Roberto Burle Marx in Guaratiba. The wall is topped with many genera of bromeliads, and jets drop water from above with a flourish.
OPPOSITE BOTTOM: A river runs through a tropical garden by Roberto Burle Marx in Rio de Janeiro. It passes over the distant spillway into a natural-looking swimming pool formed by a dam, the top of which is seen in the foreground. The banks are planted with clumps of Monstera deliciosa (split-leaf philodendron) and arecha catechu (betel nut palm).

The moist, tropical heat of Brazil's winter contrasts with the dry and equally hot summer in Spain. The serene Moorish gardens at the Alhambra in Granada celebrate the sound of water, which is so important in the harsh, dry climate. Water is the Alhambra's central theme. Pools and buildings are interlocked by watercourses. The richness of the architecture is offset by the simplicity of reflecting pools and planting. The gardens are sanctuaries, cooled by bubbling waters, splashing fountains, and gurgling rivulets.

At Expo '92 in Seville, the genius of Spanish design with water was everywhere on display. Canopies covered with *Bougainvillea* spp. (bougainvillea) hid nozzles that emitted clouds of cool mist above the pedestrians below. Large shallow pools were designed for cooling tired feet, and the watery sounds tricked one into thinking it was much cooler than the sizzling 105° F. at midday.

BELOW: At Expo '92 in Seville, water in every form of spray, cascade, and pool was featured in the shade of open pavilions. On this hot afternoon in August a visitor walks through a cooling spray of water coming up from nozzles set in the terrace. OPPOSITE: David Hockney, A Bigger Splash, 1967. Acrylic on canvas. 96" x 96". © David Hockney. OVERLEAF: A swimming pool that looks like a natural pond is the focal point of this California garden designed by Thomas D. Church. The rocks are river-washed sandstone, the plants are native and low-maintenance, and the color of the pool basin is black.
CAROLYN CADDES PHOTOGRAPH

A good way to see the contrasting sources that inspire my designs is to juxtapose the paintings of Monet and David Hockney. Giverny, the garden that Claude Monet painted in all its romantic, quiet splendor, epitomizes the importance and radiance of water in the garden. It's easy to summon liquid images of Monet's Japanese footbridge, the masses of lilies, the reflections of the weeping willows, and the rowboat tied at the bank. On the other hand, David Hockney's hard-edged pictures of California swimming pools are painted in the strong, sunlit colors of brightly glazed tile. His water reflects, splashes, sparkles—it seems almost audible in the clear California air. Both painters capture the essential movement and beauty of water.

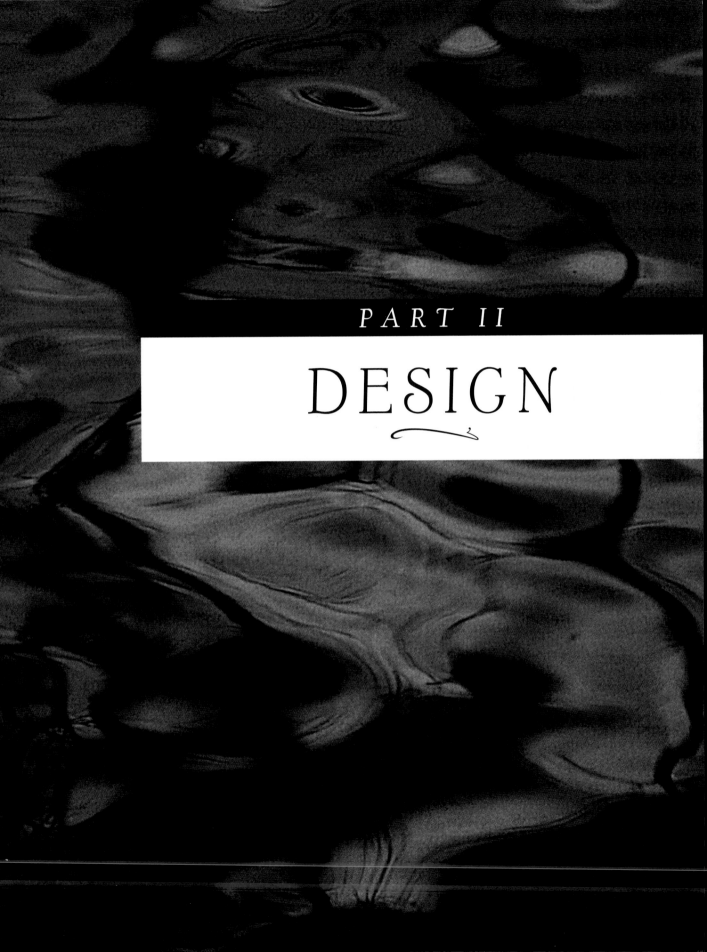

PART II

DESIGN

A P P R O A C H

Every garden can benefit from the decorative use of water. The designs featured in the following garden tour include man-made water elements, such as courtyard wall fountains and lily pools, swimming pools, recirculating waterfalls, and even dry streams in the Japanese tradition. The gardens are located in towns, suburbs, and in the countryside. Whenever possible, I incorporate "borrowed scenery," such as bay, river, or pond edges in my design.

Budget often determines how elaborate or simple a design will be. There are many varieties of construction materials for elements such as coping, retaining walls, containers, and lighting, and the choice of materials will depend on your budget. Simple and less expensive materials often are the most beautiful and enduring.

I begin the design of a water feature by first taking into account the client's needs. But my real starting point is always personal experience. We all want our gardens to be stimulating and relaxing, and to provide seclusion. Most of us enjoy touching and listening to water. Its sound revives me and often makes me nostalgic. I find that the sight of a dramatic water's edge expands and con-

OPPOSITE RIGHT: Panicum virgatum (switch grass) creates a smoky silhouette against the waterfall at Pershing Park on Pennsylvania Avenue in Washington, D.C.

PRECEDING PAGE, OPPOSITE LEFT, & LEFT:
ROGER FOLEY PHOTOGRAPHS

nects the garden to a larger world, while intricate detail ensures that the closer I look, the more interesting the scene will be.

A water feature should be large enough to inhabit the garden space in proper proportion. Such proportion is a personal preference, which ultimately must be determined through experience and the study of other gardening traditions. My travels in Japan reversed my opinion concerning the size of lily pools in a garden. It is not unusual for a lily pool in Japan to occupy one third of the garden space. Now I am convinced it is important to err on the side of too large. My first trip to Japan taught me that the bigger the pool, the better the garden.

I have also found that garden elements such as terraces, pools, and planting beds appear much larger on a drawing than when they are laid out on the site, and that planters and containers in the water take up more space than you might think. An adjacent terrace, for example, should be generous enough to balance the pool's size and shape and to accommodate furniture such as chaise longues, dining tables, and chairs. Remember that guests will gravitate toward water during parties. Again, my rule is always to err on the larger side.

The shape of your water feature depends on your taste and the requirements of your specific garden. A pool should remain in character with its surroundings. There are many shapes to choose from: a formal rectangle or oval or an informal pool with a curved, rocky edge like a natural pond. I think that formal pools with clean, symmetrical lines tend to be most appropriate for small urban sites in close proximity to the house. Curved lines will make a small space look smaller. In a large garden a formal pool shape such as a rectangle or ellipse on axis with the house "pulls" the architecture of the house into the garden. The example of this design approach on a grand scale is Versailles; but I used the same principle in the small Evans Town Garden (page 98).

I think informal pools are most appropriate on large properties, where they can be placed far from the house and relate more to nature and the garden than to the architecture of the house. A good example of this approach is the Jacobs Garden (page 38). I placed the Jacobses' pools at the edge of the woods in the distance to enhance the view from the living room and bedroom. Natural-looking pools relate to the garden and woods rather than to the house. My hope is that they look as though they have always been there. This is pure theater.

Many factors affect the location of water features on this tour. The most important are legal restrictions, topography, sunlight, view lines, and availability of utilities.

Legal restrictions are crucial and should not be overlooked. Before I begin to site a pond or pool, I investigate setback requirements and size limits. I obtain the local building code from the appropriate jurisdiction office. The code often limits pool placement, size, and depth. Do your homework now; it can save time and energy later.

I have found that using the topography of a site wisely can add immensely to the beauty of the design. I look for the elements of the land that can only be described as its genius. This can be a gentle slope into which a pond can be nestled or a steep slope that inspires a rugged waterfall. If the land rises as it recedes from the house, the water feature should be low and in the foreground so it remains in view. A waterfall cascading toward the house will add drama and white-water sound. If the land slopes away from the house, I would place a lily pool at the top near the house and terrace. You can see this in the garden on page 72. If the property is large, I would design a pond as large as possible in the distance at the bottom of the slope. You can see an example of this in the Robinson Garden on page 48. If the land is flat or the pool is placed on a level terrace, the design possibilities are infinite. For instance, in the Evans Garden on page 98, the mirrorlike flatness and geometric shape of the pool fools the eye into thinking that the garden is larger than it actually is.

Regardless of the character of the land, I take great care when grading around the pool so that the water drains away from all edges. Garden chemicals are toxic to fish, and you should avoid allowing mud to wash into the pool during heavy rains.

Sunlight is very important when I site a pool, because all of my designs feature water plants. Water lilies need a minimum of six hours of sunlight; below this threshold they will scarcely bloom. I can't imagine a pool in July without water lilies in full bloom, so I place the pool as far away from trees as possible and never on the north side of woods. Also, falling leaves increase the maintenance, and tree roots can damage the shell or liner.

I place the water feature in such a way that my clients can benefit the most from the sound and cooling of the water close by. Water sounds soothing and screens out unwanted noise. In the garden on page 127, I designed a cascade just below the bedroom window that the clients claim lulls them to sleep and helps mask the city and airplane noises in Washington, D.C. The cooling effect of water and plants is most obvious if the water is next to a terrace or deck. Evaporating water lowers the air temperature, making hot summer nights more bearable.

One last, very important point: before I begin I survey the site to ensure that utilities such as water, storm sewer, and electricity are available. I also determine how accessible the site is for both construction and maintenance. Water from the house is needed to fill and maintain the pool's or pond's water level. Electricity is required to run pumps, filters, and lighting. Concrete and dump trucks must have access to the site during construction. Of course, we have dug pools by hand where machines could not go and used the resulting soil for mounds and planters.

FOLLOWING PAGE: The circular lily pool in the Simon and Rosita Trinca Garden catches mottled reflections of an early morning sky through the canopies of giant trees.
RICHARD FELBER PHOTOGRAPH

A GARDEN TOUR

A DRY STREAM WITH FOUNTAIN
INSPIRED BY JAPAN
THE BARBARA BOLLING WOODWARD GARDEN

———

The Nicholas and Sheila Platt Garden

POOLS AT A WOODLAND EDGE
THE JACOBS GARDEN

———

The Oliver Wedgwood/Ronald Noe Garden

———

Japan Meets America in New England

———

STILL POND
THE ROBINSON GARDEN

———

CASCADE AND ESPLANADE
IN MANHATTAN
BATTERY PARK CITY AUTHORITY

———

The Carole and Alex Rosenberg Garden

———

A REFLECTIVE POOL IN A SUBURBAN GLADE
THE WENDELL AND DOROTHY HESTER GARDEN

———

WATER CROWNS A GARDEN SLOPE

———

The Maija Hay Garden

———

A PLANTSMAN'S WATER GARDEN
THE OEHME GARDEN

———

The German-American Friendship Garden

———

ROCK RIM PONDS
THE CASTAGNA REAL ESTATE COMPANY

———

Twin Bridges

AN ELLIPTICAL POOL IN A TOWN SETTING
THE EVANS GARDEN

———

The Jerald J. Littlefield Garden, Virginia

———

A TERRESTRIAL SEA ON
CHESAPEAKE BAY
THE CORBIN AND JEAN GWALTNEY GARDEN

———

Dancing Point

———

POOLS AND CASCADE IN A RAVINE
THE JOHN AND SUSAN ULFELDER GARDEN

———

The Mr. and Mrs. Edwin Hamowy Garden

———

The Mr. and Mrs. Abraham L. Adler Garden

———

WATERFALL AND POOL IN THE
CAPITAL CITY
PENNSYLVANIA AVENUE
DEVELOPMENT CORPORATION

———

The Bennett/Born Garden

———

The Paul L. Houts, Jan Munhall-Houts Garden

———

WATERFALL IN THE WOODS
THE SHOCKEY GARDEN

———

The David E. Rust Garden

———

The Simon and Rosita Trinca Garden

———

Paradise Manor

———

A HILLTOP LILY POOL WITH A WATERFALL
THE JERALD J. LITTLEFIELD GARDEN, MARYLAND

A Dry Stream
with Fountain
Inspired by
Japan

∽

THE BARBARA BOLLING
WOODWARD GARDEN

*T*his is my favorite example of what I call a "railroad-car garden" because of its long, rectangular shape defined by fences. Located in Washington, D.C.'s historic Georgetown, the town-house garden is barely seventeen feet wide, but extends some eighty feet back from the rear entrance of the house to the fence at the far end of the narrow property. From the house you can see the garden tilt slightly upward toward the back. I like to work with this configuration; from the house the elements of the garden can be viewed as if they were actors and scenery on a raked stage.

I took a design approach to this garden that is very Japanese in spirit, using water in both real and symbolic contexts. A dry streambed of randomly placed stones descends from a "pool" of stones at the elevated rear of the garden in a meandering path to the house. Midway along its run, the dry stream encounters a sculptured stone fountain with water bubbling

TOP: *A triangular pattern of dark stain is the unexpected result of water spilling over the pinwheel-shaped stone fountain.*
BOTTOM: *The dry streambed ends in a "pool" of stepping stones cut into a terrace off the sitting room. Mazus reptans 'Alba' (white mazus) fills the joints between the stones.*
OPPOSITE: *A pink granite fountain in the shape of a millstone is the centerpiece of this garden. It is seen here from the house in midsummer, framed by Lagerstroemia indica 'Natchez' (crepe myrtle 'Natchez'). The fountain is placed at midpoint along a dry stream of stone, which can be seen in the foreground. Wrapping around the back is Hosta x 'Honeybells' (lavender plantain lily), and in front is Coreopsis verticillata 'Moonbeam' (cutleaf tickseed).*

from its center. The stream terminates in another "pool" of stones cut into a garden terrace adjacent to the house. The three dry pools in the sequence break up the long, narrow garden and visually foreshorten the space.

A shaded sitting area at the far end of the garden is the "source" of the dry stream. A circular arrangement of stones mimics a watery pool from which the stone stream emerges and starts its descent to the house. The fountain at the midpoint of the stream is made of pink granite and shaped like a millstone. It was quarried and hand-carved in Asia. Water gushes from a hole in the center of the stone and washes its surface and the surrounding stones on the ground. It then disappears into a hidden reservoir below. The top of the stone is carved in the shape of a pinwheel. As water pours over the edge, a beautifully scalloped pattern of stain emerges where the surface of the stone is alternately wet and dry. In summer, the soothing sounds of water bubbling from the fountain and dripping onto the surrounding stones serenade the whole garden. In winter, when the water is turned off, the fountain becomes a powerful stone sculpture. When the water is left on during frigid months, playful ice sculpture emerges.

wood fence

The fountain is particularly intriguing because there is no visible pool of standing water at its base. The hidden reservoir from which the water recirculates lies beneath rocks and a steel grate beneath the sculpture. The necessary mechanical parts—the pump and overflow—are concealed below the surface of what appears to be a natural stone cover. A trapdoor in the lid gives access to the pool and mechanical equipment. For convenience, the pump is activated by a switch inside the house.

I designed this garden in collaboration with the owner, Barbara Bolling Woodward. We are both interested in Japanese design and have visited Japan often. The dry stream, the understated use of water

NORTH

0   5   10   15 feet

at the fountain, and the simple interstices of quiet space where one can pause and be washed over by the beauty of the garden—each element reflects the Japanese spirit and transforms what was once an awkward urban space into a calm retreat.

Fountain bubbler

Granite millstone

Water recirculates from the
fountain across the face of the
millstone onto riverstones, through
metal grate into the pool

River stone on cast iron grate

Brick base supports millstone

water flow control valve
(access through concealed
opening in grate)

Submersible pump

Water line to fountain

Overflow pipe

Reinforced-concrete pool wall

Stoneyhurst flagstone
in pea gravel

Millstone fountain

Terrace

House

I designed this town garden for clients who share my love of Japan. The confined space is a perfect setting for design in the Japanese spirit. The Platts call it their Tokyo garden. The garden steps upward from the terrace level at the house to a weathered brick wall at the back property line, where I placed a small fountain on the elevated ground. From the house the fountain appears to be at eye level and subtly focuses the attention. Visitors approach it along a garden path that rises on massive stone steps from the terrace.

The fountain is limestone carved in the cylindrical shape of a millstone. Its form is remi-

THE NICHOLAS AND SHEILA PLATT GARDEN

niscent of the Japanese *tsukubai*, a water basin used in the purification ceremony before tea. The stone has a hole in the center from which a small jet of water erupts. A quarter-inch lip around the outer edge retains a shallow surface of reflective water. Concentric ripples of water from the jet overflow from the lip and wash over the side of the cylinder before splashing onto a bed of river-washed stones at ground level. The stones sit on an iron grate above a hidden reservoir of recirculating water. The garden path extends the water as a "dry stream" from the base of the fountain to the terrace "pool" below.

Birds are attracted to the sparkling, musical water in the Platt Garden and frequently come to the water's edge to drink and bathe. They add an unexpected dimension year-round to the contemplative landscape.

Volkmar K. Wentzel photograph

Pools at a
Woodland Edge

THE JACOBS GARDEN

*T*his elegant suburban estate is a gardener's delight. When I want to show a garden that combines water with other landscape elements to create a single beautiful statement, this is a favorite subject. Fortunately, the Jacobses allow frequent visits.

Water is indirectly the star of this show, not so much the focal point as a sparkling foil to the exquisitely detailed and maintained surroundings. The garden was developed in two stages, the first being designed by landscape architect Lester Collins. There are multilevel terraces, immaculate pavements and retaining walls, broad stairs, intricate fences and gates, a pergola, swimming pool, rivers of lawn, and soft masses of perennial plants and ornamental grasses. Raised cutting beds yield flowers, fruit, and foliage for Mrs. Jacobs's professional flower arranging and add to the parklike atmosphere. A mature woodland frames the pristine core of the property.

The water site virtually selected itself. A setting at the edge of the woods that could be viewed from the master-bedroom wing and main outdoor-living terrace invited water. It was a natural site for a stream.

I sited two pools, one raised above the other, at the base of an opening in the woods. The topography falls perceptibly from the forest floor down to the edge of the lawn. A generous waterfall connects the pools and creates an illusory "stream" that is reinforced by randomly placed boulders trailing upstream and downstream through the woods. I defined the pools and waterfall with massive stones arranged as natural formations.

PRECEDING SPREAD: *Two pools placed midway in a gentle slope provide a pleasing transition from woodland to lawn. Shown here in spring, the pools reinforce the imagery of a stream emerging from the woods. The placement of rocks, the lawn edge at the far side, and the generous size of the pools show the Japanese influence.*

LEFT: *Looking "upstream," water falls over rocks into the larger of two pools. The full blossoming of* Cornus florida *(American dogwood) and* Rhododendron spp. *add authenticity to the woodland stream imagery.*

OPPOSITE: *Looking toward the house, the garden steps up to the patio where terraces of yellow* Hemerocallis spp. *(daylilies) flourish.* Typha angustifolio *and* Pontederia cordata *are growing at the foreground edge of the upper pool and* Sagittaria spp. *on the opposite side.*

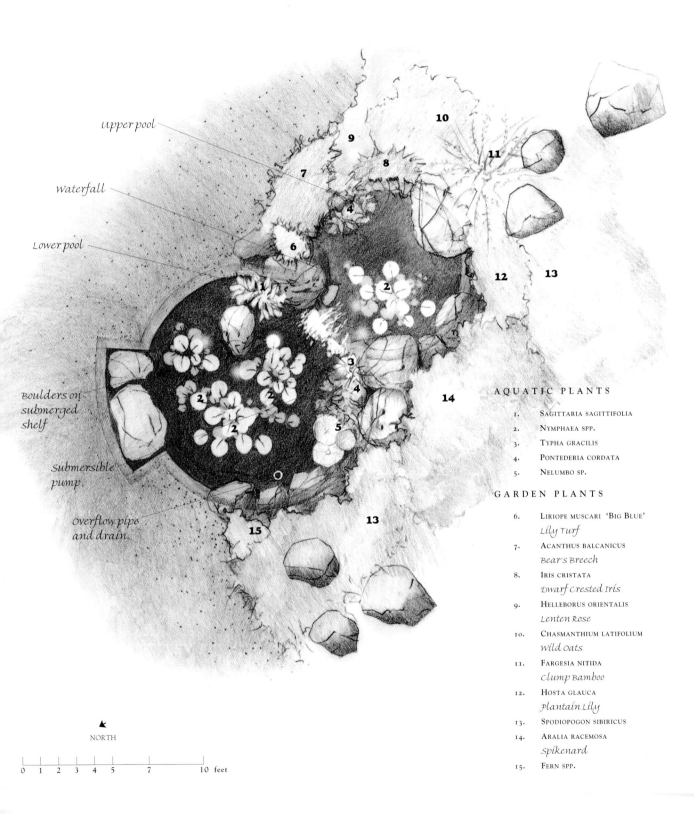

upper pool

waterfall

Lower pool

Boulders on
submerged
shelf

Submersible
pump

Overflow pipe
and drain

NORTH

0	1	2	3	4	5	7	10 feet

AQUATIC PLANTS

1. SAGITTARIA SAGITTIFOLIA

2. NYMPHAEA SPP.

3. TYPHA GRACILIS

4. PONTEDERIA CORDATA

5. NELUMBO SP.

GARDEN PLANTS

6. LIRIOPE MUSCARI 'BIG BLUE'
   Lily Turf

7. ACANTHUS BALCANICUS
   Bear's Breech

8. IRIS CRISTATA
   Dwarf Crested Iris

9. HELLEBORUS ORIENTALIS
   Lenten Rose

10. CHASMANTHIUM LATIFOLIUM
    Wild Oats

11. FARGESIA NITIDA
    Clump Bamboo

12. HOSTA GLAUCA
    Plantain Lily

13. SPODIOPOGON SIBIRICUS

14. ARALIA RACEMOSA
    Spikenard

15. FERN SPP.

Also, an "invisible" pool wall allows the lawn on the near side to end abruptly in a sharp line at the water's edge.

The illusion of a stream was easy to create because of the site's natural features, its topography, and linear opening into the woods, and by the generous sizes of the pools. The dimensions of the pools teach an important lesson—they are large. My rule of thumb is that pools can be too small, but can never be too large, even in smaller gardens. Timid dimensions here would have spoiled the illusion and compromised the natural appearance.

The lawn areas of the garden, laid out like flowing ribbons but with sharply defined edges, subtly enhance the watery theme. The lawn resembles a river that emerges in a wide sweep from the higher elevations at the front of the house, converges with the illusory stream just below the waterfall, then continues its descent along the rest of the garden.

I designed the Jacobses' pools soon after my first trip to Japan. The Japanese influence erupts in the placement of stones around the oversized pools, the dry stream of rocks, and the quiet pooling of water at the edge of the woods. The composition is all theater. Its role is to soothe the senses and to announce "This is Nature."

Blooming in the foreground is Sagittaria sagittifolia, with its beautiful heart-shaped leaves and white flowers; just below the surface are the tiny white flowers of Elodea canadensis; and in the distance on the right are the delicate leaves of Fargesia nitida (clump bamboo).

This tiny "room garden" overflows with visual delights and design lessons. In addition to the small fountain, it consists of a short garden path, a small sitting terrace, and a collection of plants that emerge from every available ground surface, including containers. The spontaneous and casual effect is a response to my concern that gardens of this intimate scale often appear overdesigned.

The fountain design is equally understated. It is a simple stone

THE OLIVER WEDGWOOD/ RONALD NOE GARDEN

dish that appears to float like a piece of sculpture above a slightly raised bed of river-washed stones. A bubbler in the center of the dish sends just enough water over the rounded edge of the dish to create a soft musical sound as it falls onto the stones. An underground reservoir collects the water for recirculation.

The fountain's comforting musical presence draws attention to itself, even from inside the house, just as a fireplace charms a comfortable room.

ROGER FOLEY PHOTOGRAPH

A renovated New England wood frame house in a historic village of suburban Boston is an unlikely setting for these dramatic reminiscences of Japan. The owners travel extensively in Japan and share my strong affinity with the quiet simplicity of Japanese gardens.

A large lily pool adds theatrical impact to the design. I nestled the pool in a narrow space between the exterior glass walls of the sunroom and a beautiful outcropping of natural rock. When approached from the outdoors, the pool is the primary destination of a rambling walkway through woodland gardens that encircle the entire house. When viewed from the house, it is a dramatic visual extension of the living environment.

The Japanese design spirit is most evident in the treatment of the pool's edges, especially the detailing of stone work. Next to the glass wall, an overhanging bluestone ledge

Japan Meets America in New England

sharply defines the edge of the pool. The ledge is just wide enough to serve as part of the perimeter walkway. The ledge terminates at a small sitting terrace opposite the kitchen. Note especially how a narrow band of gravel at the outer edges of this terrace provides a subtle transition from pool coping of rough-cut granite to the geometrically coursed pattern of bluestone pavers. A surface of granite stones extends the sitting terrace to a rich palette of shade perennial plantings. Boulders placed as sculpture in the water at the far end of the pool enhance the natural look and add foreground interest for the plants. Finally, the opposite edge of the pool is defined in dramatic fashion by natural rock outcroppings that rise abruptly from the surface of the water.

A bridge of stepping-stones provides a final touch of whimsy as it crosses the pool from the sitting terrace. From its landing on the opposite side, random stone steps ascend between the rocks and through beautiful stands of mature native trees to a quiet resting place.

Still Pond

THE ROBINSON
GARDEN

The Robinsons' garden was carefully crafted in the midst of a magnificent setting from a unique program of requirements. The setting is a large horse farm in the rolling foothills of the Blue Ridge Mountains in central Virginia. The foreground is an expanse of undulating pastureland, randomly framed by forests. Intermittent "windows" in the forests allow longer views and intensify the sense of spaciousness. The majestic panorama of the Blue Ridge mountain range provides a mutable backdrop. In this project, Wolfgang and I tried to respect the spectacular surroundings and design a garden that quietly complements but does not compete with the scenery.

Program requirements were unusual and challenging. First, since the property is an active horse farm, my design treats the house and its immediate environment as an integral part of the pasture scene, not as an island apart. Horses come close to the house, where a ha-ha (a wall of stone or wood embedded in a slope to create an "invisible" barrier between pasture and lawn) tricks the eye into thinking there are no fences at all. In addition to keeping horses, the Robinsons have an active social and family life, a keen interest in wildlife, and a sophisticated knowledge of plants. The garden is totally accessible to a family member who is physically disabled. The design accommodates a motorized wheelchair and permits active participation in the care and maintenance of ponds, plants, and wildlife.

As one approaches the house along the picturesque drive, a farm pond appears suddenly in a small valley opposite the main entrance to the house. A continuous system of

PRECEDING SPREAD: *Approaching the house, the farm pond surrounded by planting appears in a small valley. A system of boardwalks and paths encircles the pond and links it to the rest of the garden. The gazebo is a shady respite along the way.*

LEFT: *The distant Blue Ridge Mountains cap a dramatic view progression from the lily pool, swimming pool, and newly planted garden. The pergola seen at the right side of the swimming-pool terrace is a summer gathering place for family and friends.*

OPPOSITE: *The majestic panorama of the mountains is framed here by forests and Miscanthus sinensis 'Malepartus' (silver grass). On the far side of the swimming pool, Pennisetum alopecuroides (fountain grass) and Sedum telephium 'Autumn Joy' (stonecrop) are planted right up to the coping.*
ROGER FOLEY PHOTOGRAPHS

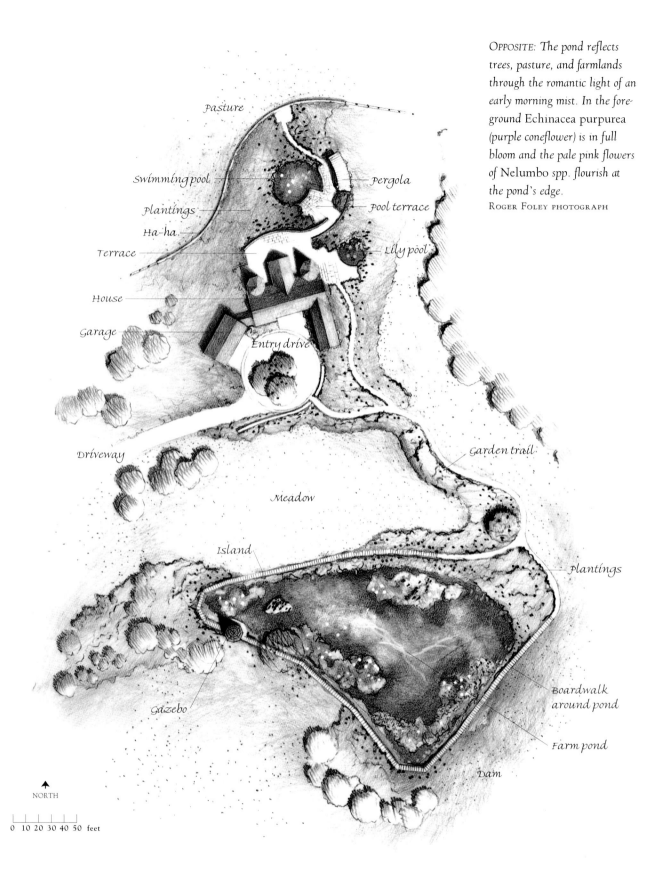

Pasture

Swimming pool

Plantings

Ha-ha

Terrace

House

Garage

Driveway

Pergola

Pool terrace

Lily pool

Entry drive

Garden trail

Meadow

Plantings

Island

Boardwalk
around pond

Gazebo

Farm pond

Dam

NORTH

0 10 20 30 40 50 feet

paths and boardwalks links the pond to the rest of the water environment, including the swimming pool on the opposite side of the house and a lily pool. One can pause along the path to sit in the gazebo by the pond, the pergola near the swimming pool, or at the ha-ha at the edge of the pasture where horses occasionally turn up. There a small terrace overlooks the mountain scene, gardens, and specimen plants.

The farm pond was in place when we began the project, so we used several techniques to give it an established look. A cleverly sculpted dam nestled at the lower end of the valley appears to be a natural earth form. Plantings emerge from the water's edge and spread to surrounding slopes and pastures. The boardwalk, which encircles the edge of the pond, meanders among the plantings and sometimes disappears completely. Finally, the pond reflects the native and newly introduced trees that surround and anchor it firmly to its site. The sounds of bullfrogs and geese from the small offshore island complete the scene.

A boardwalk encircles the pond, meandering through plantings that emerge from the water's edge and spread up the slope to the house.

ROGER FOLEY PHOTOGRAPH

GARDEN PLANTS

1. ASTER NOVAE ANGLIAE 'ALMA POETSCHKE'
   New England Aster
2. SEDUM 'AUTUMN JOY'
   Stonecrop
3. PENNISETUM ALOPECUROIDES
   Fountain Grass
4. HIBISCUS MOSCHEUTOS 'ANNE ARUNDEL'
   Pink Rose Mallow
5. VERONICA LONGIFOLIA 'SUNNY BORDER BLUE'
   Blue Veronica
6. COREOPSIS VERTICILLATA 'MOONBEAM'
   Yellow Tickseed
   with
   LIATRIS SPICATA
   Gayfeather
   and
   PEROVSKIA ATRIPLICIFOLIA
   Russian Sage
7. PANICUM VIRGATUM 'ROTSTRAHLBUSCH'
   Red Witch Grass
8. CERCIDIPHYLLUM JAPONICUM
   Katsura Tree
9. ASTER LATERIFLORUS 'HORIZONTALIS'
10. CLADRASTIS LUTEA
    American Yellowwood
11. RUDBECKIA MAXIMA
    Coneflower
12. MONARDA DIDYMA 'CAMBRIDGE SCARLET'
    Bergamot
13. STOKESIA LAEVIS "BLUE DANUBE"
    Blue Stokesia
14. COTONEASTER SALICIFOLIA
    Cotoneaster
15. MOLINIA CAERULEA 'WINDSPIEL'
    Purple Moor Grass—(PLANTED UNDER TREE)
16. FRANKLINIA ALATAMAHA
    Franklin Tree
17. LIRIOPE MUSCARI 'BIG BLUE'
    Lilyturf
18. FARGESIA NITIDA
    Clump Bamboo
19. ACER GRISEUM
    Paperbark Maple
20. SALVIA SUPERBA
    Blue Salvia
21. HIBISCUS MOSCHEUTOS 'LORD BALTIMORE'
22. SPODIOPOGON SIBIRICA
    Silver Spike Grass
23. PANICUM VIRGATUM 'HAENSE HERMS'

AQUATIC PLANTS

24. NYMPHAEA SPP.
25. THALIA DEALBATA
26. IRIS PSEUDACORUS
27. NELUMBO SPP.
28. PONTEDERIA CORDATA

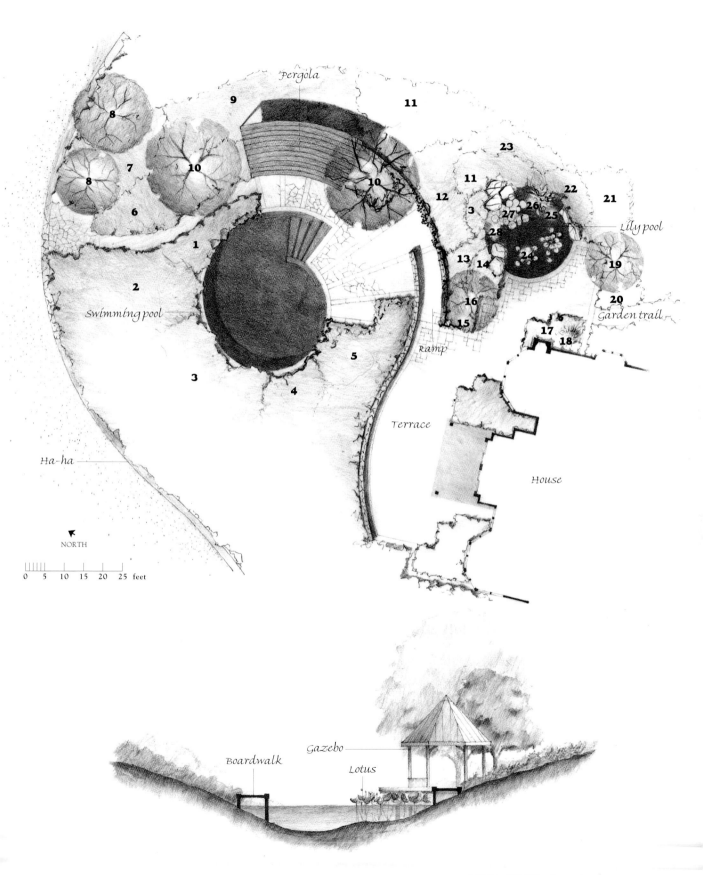

Pergola

9

11

8

23

7   10

11

8   10   12   22

6   3   26   21

1   27 25   Lily pool

28

2   13   24

Swimming pool   14   19

16   20

5   15   Garden trail

3   17   16

4   18

Ramp

Terrace

House

Ha-ha

NORTH

0   5   10   15   20   25 feet

Boardwalk   Gazebo

Lotus

A gazebo by the boardwalk on the pond's far side is a shady refuge where the Robinsons and guests often relax in the late afternoon. Mrs. Robinson even uses the seasonal variations in water elevation to advantage: when the level is low, the exposed "ring" becomes a racetrack for her dog.

I sited the swimming pool and its terrace in their own world on the "view" side of the house, about eighteen inches lower than the main terrace. By stepping down the pool and terrace, carefully laying out the ha-has, and planting up to the pool on one side, we managed to pull the pasture right up to the house. From the terrace, it appears as if the horses could come drink directly from the pool.

I designed the pool to mirror the shape of a chambered nautilus. Its perfect spiral extends the overarching design and reflects the sweeps and curves of the natural sur-

ROGER FOLEY PHOTOGRAPH

roundings. It also provides easy ramp access and movement within the pool for the physically disabled.

The lily pool is the final event of the water tour. It is a fascinating interlude; a place to enjoy fish and aquatic plants. Its uphill relationship to both swimming pool and farm pond adds three-dimensional interest and implies that the waters connect. Plantings overhang the waterline and boulders obscure the circular shape of the pool edge. The pool wall is beveled on top, leaving only a very thin line of concrete exposed.

The Robinsons asked us to design a garden that is sympathetic to their pastoral surroundings and responsive to their hobbies, interests, and special needs. The garden, I think, is worthy of the name they chose for it: Still Pond.

Cascade and
Esplanade in
Manhattan

BATTERY PARK CITY
AUTHORITY

Hudson River Park is the largest public open space in New York's Battery Park City. The eight-acre park, built on landfill in the Hudson River, is a celebration of the modern metropolis and a gesture of respect for the beach environment that flourished on the site centuries ago. Its human scale is a welcome relief at the edge of the city. New Yorkers are comfortable with the classical design of the park; romantic vistas of lawns, meadows, and water remind them of Central Park. Stone walls and ornamental pavement add a sense of permanence.

PRECEDING SPREAD: *The broad esplanade along the Hudson River edge is designed for the enjoyment of people who live and work in lower Manhattan in New York City. Here they can get close to the water for fishing, promenading, and taking in fresh ocean air.*
ABOVE: *A cascading crescent of water anchors the park on the south and welcomes visitors to a lively crossroads event at the end of Vesey Street.*
OPPOSITE: *Looking south over the great lily pool with water cascading from its elevated bowl, the white peaks of the Hoboken ferry terminal and the Statue of Liberty are clearly visible in the morning light.*

A great lily pool with a crescent of cascading water from an elevated bowl anchors the south end of the park. The pool is a crossroads event at the end of Vesey Street. The overlook terrace above the cascade is a gathering place for park visitors. The strong visual relationship between the pool and the river is most compelling from this vantage point; the rush of water over the cascade and the reflective waters of the pool introduce the river as a principal attraction.

The pool's rich materials and careful detailing reinforce the classical image of the park. The elevated bowl is granite with a river-stone edge, the coping at the edge of the pool is black granite, and the walls are ashlar. The shell of the pool is formed concrete and the water recirculates through a sophisticated system of filters, skimmers, and returns.

A fascinating collection of water plants adds life to the pool. Examples include *Iris pseudacorus*, *Nymphaea* spp., *Pontederia cordata*, *Thalia dealbata*, and *Sagittaria lancifolia* (arrowhead). Special construction details ensure the plants' survival. A plastic baffle calms the water beneath the cascade so that lilies can grow in the center of the pool. A heavy mulch of pea gravel anchors custom-built wood and steel planters to the pool floor. Plants overwinter in the containers that remain in place throughout the year.

Battery Park City officials wanted a "seaside quality" of planting along the esplanade at the river's edge. My inspiration for the planting came from an earlier garden for Alex and Carole Rosenberg on Mecox Bay, Long Island, New York. The plant palette I chose respects both the native Hudson River valley landscape and the Long Island shoreline beach environment.

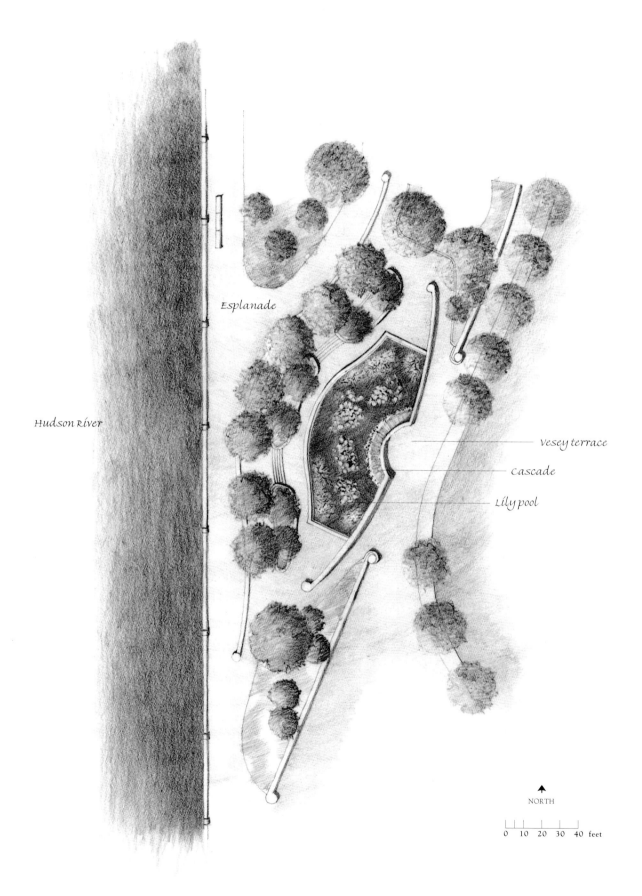

Hudson River

Esplanade

Vesey terrace

Cascade

Lily pool

NORTH

					feet
0	10	20	30	40	

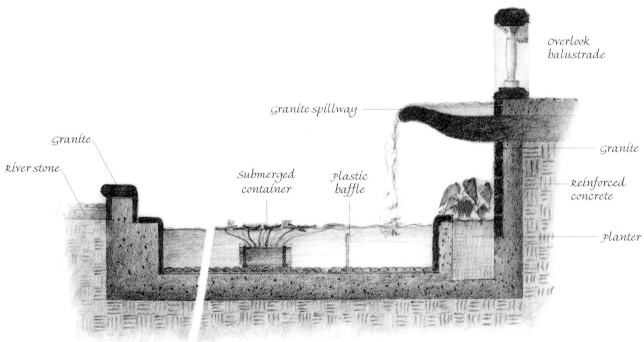

Overlook
balustrade

Granite spillway

Granite

River stone

Granite

Reinforced
concrete

Submerged
container

Plastic
baffle

Planter

Cutline

An extraordinary backdrop of natural scenery inspired our design for the Carole and Alex Rosenberg Garden at their weekend retreat on Long Island's Mecox Bay. Permanently etched in my mind is my first glimpse of the bay, with its shimmering expanse of water, its undulating islands of marsh grasses, and the immense sky that anticipates the open sea, just beyond view. No artificial boundaries exist here; the foreground simply melts into the distant panorama of this romantic bay edge.

The challenge in designing the garden was to create a distinctive foreground that would complement the extended scene. Wolfgang and I added great horizontal masses of *Miscanthus sinensis condensatus* (purple-blooming Japanese silver grass) at the water's edge, complementing the sweeps of *Phragmites australis* (com-

THE CAROLE AND ALEX ROSENBERG GARDEN

mon reed) in the distance. A small, fluid lawn leads the eye to the water's edge and allows a full view of the bay from various points in and around the house. The flat plane of the lawn seems to invite the bay right into the living space. Water views were supplemented with unexpected glimpses of the bay from other garden spaces. The perennial borders and overhanging branches of trees frame the distant views and add dimension. The resulting garden is lively and delightful and lends even more resonance to the spectacular scenery that lies beyond.

As connoisseurs and dealers of art on an international scale, the Rosenbergs insisted that their garden also be a work of art. The garden at Mecox Bay perfectly expresses their artistic interests, their appreciation of nature, and their shared passion for gardening.

RICHARD FELBER PHOTOGRAPH

A Reflective
Pool in a
Suburban Glade

∼

THE WENDELL AND
DOROTHY HESTER
GARDEN

This large suburban property contained a wealth of natural qualities: interesting topography; mature tree cover; a house set at the top of a wooded slope overlooking a golf course in the valley below; living areas extended to the outdoors on secluded decks; foreground views of undisturbed woods; and contrasting "borrowed" views of the manicured golf course in the background. Water was the only missing element. The owner and I quickly agreed to create a lily pool of generous proportions as the garden's centerpiece.

The pool site and its terrace is a broad plateau on the slope between the house and the edge of the golf course. Since natural water features did not exist on the site, my main challenge was to create a pool that would appear to be part of the natural environment. I used a number of techniques to achieve this. First, the size of the pool was important. I designed pool and terrace to occupy the entire plateau. Second, I created visual uncertainty about the pool's exact boundaries by carefully locating boulders like natural outcroppings and masses of plants to obscure the water's edge, except on the near side where the sharp terrace edge appears to float above the water like a bridge. The eye tends to exaggerate the extent and form of the water's surface (the pool is perfectly elliptical). To further erode the edge, some boulders are partially submerged on the pool side and cut into the slightly elevated terrace on the other side.

Finally, Wolfgang selected and placed plants to reinforce the natural look. The lines of merger are indistinguishable as water plants blend first

Preceding Spread & Opposite:
The etchings of winter expose the "bones" of the garden. Water reflects the spare look of the season while the pale colors of dried leaves intermittently soften sharp structural edges.
Right: Steps from the house cascade to the terrace and lily pool. Except for the sharp curve of the terrace edge, the side of this perfectly elliptical pool is eroded by lush plantings and boulders. In the foreground is
Agapanthus *'Blue Triumphator' (lily of the Nile) and* Molinia arundinaceae *'Windspiel' (tall purple moor grass).*

into newly introduced plants around the pool and then with the native plants in the woods beyond. The soft continuum of plant masses originates in the pool and spills into its surroundings. He chose plants for their seasonal interest to maintain the effect throughout the year.

Small details add life to the watery theme: a carefully placed fountain bubbler sends ripples across the open surface of the water and entertains with its soft gurgling sound. Broad stone stairs cascade from the house to the pool terrace; landings along the way appear to be dry "pools." Garden paths meander like streams around the house before converging at the pool.

Opportunities for enjoying this pool abound. I enjoy sampling them all: sitting high above on the terrace with its commanding view; moving down the grand cascade of steps to poolside; and strolling into the woods, where more views and natural surprises await.

AQUATIC PLANTS

1. THALIA DEALBATA
2. NYMPHAEA SPP.
3. IRIS PSEUDACORUS
4. NELUMBO SP.

GARDEN PLANTS

5. FERNS SPP.
6. HOSTA SP.
7. ACER PALMATUM
   Japanese Maple
8. PENNISETUM ALOPECUROIDES
   Fountain Grass
9. RUDBECKIA FULGIDA 'GOLDSTURM'
   Black-eyed Susan
10. LYTHRUM SALICARIA 'MORDEN'S PINK'
    Loosestrife
11. MISCANTHUS SINENSIS PURPURASCENS
    Purple Silver Grass
12. HELIANTHUS ANGUSTIFOLIUS
13. AGAPANTHUS 'BLUE TRIUMPHATOR'
    Lily of the Nile
14. MOLINIA ARUNDINCEA CAERULEA
    'WINDSPIEL'
    Tall Purple Moor Grass
15. LOBELIA SIPHILITICA
    Blue Cardinal Flower

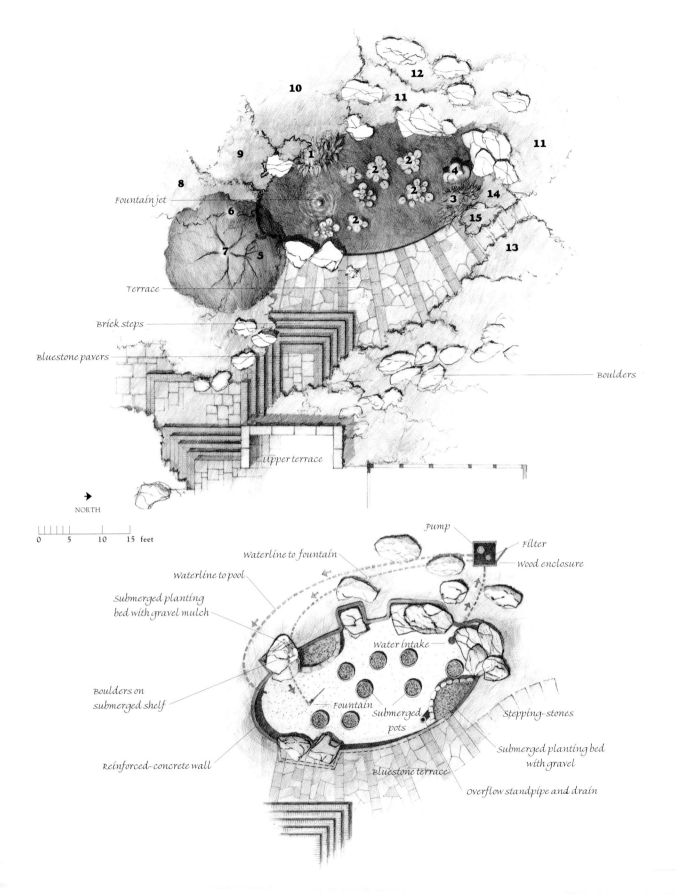

10

12

11

11

9

1

2

2

8

4

Fountain jet

2

14

6

2

3

15

7

5

2

13

Terrace

Brick steps

Bluestone pavers

Boulders

NORTH

0   5   10   15 feet

Pump

Filter

Waterline to fountain

Wood enclosure

Waterline to pool

Submerged planting
bed with gravel mulch

Water intake

Boulders on
submerged shelf

Fountain

Submerged
pots

Stepping-stones

Submerged planting bed
with gravel

Reinforced-concrete wall

Bluestone terrace

Overflow standpipe and drain

Upper terrace

Water Crowns
a Garden Slope

Challenging or difficult sites often bring out the best in designers and clients. This was certainly the case with this garden. The property is long and narrow and slopes steeply from front to back. The main level of the house is a "shelf" that appears to be carved out of the slope, a full story below street level. The approach to the house from the street is by stairs down a planted embankment.

The initial plan for the garden did not include water. The owner loves flowers and thought including a pool might limit the space available for plants. It was only after her visit to Wolfgang's garden, with its terraced water surfaces, that the pool became a must. "The experience caught me totally by surprise," she remembers. "I was so taken by the relationship of water and plants to the rest of the garden, I agreed immediately to add a lily pool."

I placed the pool at the back of the house, at the far edge of the "shelf." The pool "anchors" a small terrace and extends the horizontal plane of the house to the crown of the hill. Generous planting in the water and at its edge on the far side softens the transition to the garden that slopes down to the rear property line, some sixteen feet below terrace level.

Because of space and budget constraints the pool is modest in scale and simple in form—a rectangle about twelve feet by twenty feet with a notch taken out of one corner for the terrace. I concurred with the owner's opinion that the water should be still—no waterfall or fountain. "I like the quiet and stillness of the water," she says, "it draws

Preceding Spread: Back-lit by the sun, Thalia dealbata anchors the front edge of this lily pool and casts crisp shadows on the brick coping and Pennsylvania bluestone terrace.
Left & Opposite: The quiet, natural appearance of the pool is accentuated by lush growth during the summer. Generous plantings in and around the water include Typha, Pontederia , and Scirpus.
Roger Foley photograph

me out to watch it, to be near it." Since the total space for pool and terrace is small, the relationship of the two is very important; notice that the water surface is almost as large as the adjoining terrace. The balanced ratio gives the impression of greatly expanded space. The abrupt slope of the garden just beyond the far edge of the pool reinforces the illusion.

The pool terrace quickly became the center of attraction for the entire garden. It is a striking foreground feature when viewed from both levels of the house. It is also a favorite outdoor dining and sitting area in warm weather and the staging point for walking tours along meandering paths through the garden. The quiet, natural setting attracts wildlife as well, including a great blue heron who visits every year.

This garden demonstrates water's remarkable powers to command attention and add sparkle to an entire garden scene, even when it is used in modest dimensions and simple form. Water is the perfect finishing touch.

Seen from above in autumn, the pool extends the horizontal plane of the small terrace and anchors it to the crown of the hill. Generous plantings on the far side of the pool soften the transition to the hillside garden that slopes down sixteen feet in vertical elevation to the rear property line.
RICHARD FELBER PHOTOGRAPH

I designed this water garden for Maija Hay's home and pottery studio in 1978. The lily pool was the largest I had ever designed at that time. It is a vault shape, thirty-two feet across the base at the terrace. When it was finished I realized that the garden's wonderful sense of scale was due largely to the pool's dimensions. The experience was a valuable lesson in design and the basis of my proposition that a pool can never be too large.

The Maija Hay Garden

The pool draws the eye from every corner of the garden, and especially from the house and studio. The view is especially dramatic from a second-floor balcony next to the master bedroom and from the pottery studio, where students can see the pool through a glass wall.

Heavy planting obscures all but the sharp terrace edge of the water. Visitors stroll through pottery exhibits on the poolside terrace. Images of the sky and surrounding vegetation are mirrored in the dark water.

A Plantsman's Water Garden

THE OEHME GARDEN

Wolfgang is a plants person. He and I both love water, and use it as a planting medium and to reflect the surrounding landscape whenever possible. To us, the juxtaposition of water and plants adds irresistible magic to a garden. His garden is a laboratory, where he tests new and unusual plants. Many successful experiments find their way into the gardens of adventurous clients. We both like the way his garden changes seasonally as he adds new plants and removes others.

Since his garden slopes away from the back of the house, he designed it to recede in graduating horizontal planes that follow the natural contours of the land, from lily pool and swimming pool to decks and terraces. Even the boundaries of the vegetable garden at the base of the slope add to the effect. The final layer is a planting area that serves as a lush backdrop for the more structured, watery foreground.

He built the lily pool on the upper level, nearest the house. It is the focal point of the entire garden and can be seen from the master bedroom, dining room, library, and deck. A stone terrace abuts the pool on two sides where guests like to relax. The swimming pool lies a few steps below and gives the illusion that the waters connect and flow throughout the garden.

He planted the lily pool with a collection of his favorite aquatics. Raised planting beds on the floor of the pool separate the plants by size and characteristics, so that the taller and more aggressive ones, such as *Nelumbo* spp. and *Zizania* spp., don't spread and

Preceding Spread: The garden steps away from the house in planes that recede with the contours of the land. The lily pool at the top leads the eye to the swimming pool a few steps below. Visually, the waters connect, leaving the illusion that water flows throughout the garden.
Right: Wolfgang's lily pool is planted with a collection of favorite aquatics. The surfaces of underwater planting beds are raised to within eight inches of the water surface. To discourage algae growth during the hot summer months, water plants shade at least one half of the water surface.
Opposite: In autumn, the whole surface of the pool reappears from under the shade of the water plants. Seen from the terrace, the seasonal change leaves dazzling colors to obscure the pool's edge.
Richard Felber photograph

TOP: *The flowers of* Rudbeckia maxima *(native black-eyed Susan) and* Perovskia atriplicifolia *(Russian sage) appear to break the crisp edge of the swimming pool coping.*
ROGER FOLEY PHOTOGRAPHS

GARDEN PLANTS

1. EUPATORIUM PURPUREUM 'GATEWAY'
   Joe-Pye Weed
2. PANICUM VIRGATUM
   Switch Grass
3. SILPHIUM PERFOLIATUM
   Cupplant
4. HIBISCUS MOSCHEUTOS 'LORD BALTIMORE'
   Red Rose Mallow
5. MOLINEA CAERULEA 'TRANSPARENT'
   Purple Moor Grass
6. LYTHRUM SALICARIA 'MORDEN'S PINK'
   Loosestrife
7. MISCANTHUS SINENSIS 'UNDINE'
   Undine Silver Grass
8. VIBURNUM CARLESII
   Fragrant Viburnum
9. PEUCEDANUM VERTICILLARE
   Hog Fennel
10. PHYSOSTEGIA VIRGINIANA 'VIVID'
    False Dragonhead
11. RUDBECKIA MAXIMA
    Coneflower
12. VERONICA LONGIFOLIA 'SUNNY BORDER BLUE'
    Blue Veronica
13. ACANTHUS BALCANICUS
    Bear's Breech
14. ARTEMISIA LUDOVICIANA 'ALBULA'
    Wormwood
15. CHRYSANTHEMUM PACIFICUM
    Gold and Silver Chrysanthemum
16. AMELANCHIER HYBRID 'CUMULUS'
    Shadblow
17. CLERODENDRONTRICHOTOMUM FARGESII
    Harlequin Glorybower
18. CALAMINTHA NEPETOIDES
    Calamint
19. HAMAMELIS 'ARNOLD PROMISE'
    Witch Hazel
20. MISCANTHUS SINENSIS 'ROTSILBER'
    Red Silver Grass
21. PENNISETUM ALOPECUROIDES 'MOUDRY'
    Fountain Grass
22. ASTER NOVAE ANGLIAE 'ALMA POETSCHKE'
    New England Aster
23. COREOPSIS VERTICILLATA 'ZAGREB'
    Cutleaf Tickseed
24. EUPHORBIA PALUSTRIS
    Wood Spurge
25. MISCANTHUS SINENSIS GIGANTEUS
    Giant Silver Grass
    SYN. MISCANTHUS FLORIDULUS
26. LYSIMACHIA CLETHROIDES
    White Gooseneck
27. TSUGA CANANDENSIS
    Canadian Hemlock
28. RUDBECKIA FULGIDA 'GOLDSTURM'
    Black-Eyed Susan
29. BUDDLEIA ALTERNIFOLIA
    Fountain Buddleia
30. BUDDLEIA DAVIDII
    Butterfly Bush
31. INULA MAGNIFICA
    Elecampane
32. LYTHRUM SALICARIA 'MORDEN'S PINK'
    Loosestrife
33. EUONYMUS EUROPAEA
    European Spindle Tree
34. CHELONE LYONII
    Pink Turtlehead
35. MISCANTHUS SINENSIS 'ZWERGELEFANT'
    Dwarf Elephant Silver Grass

AQUATIC PLANTS

36. NELUMBO SPP.
37. TYPHA ANGUSTIFOLIA
38. SAGITTARIA LATIFOLIA
39. ZIZANIA LATIFOLIA
40. PONTEDERIA CORDATA
41. APONOGETON DISTACHYUS
42. ELODEA CANADENSIS
43. NYMPHAEA SPP.
44. THALIA DEALBATA

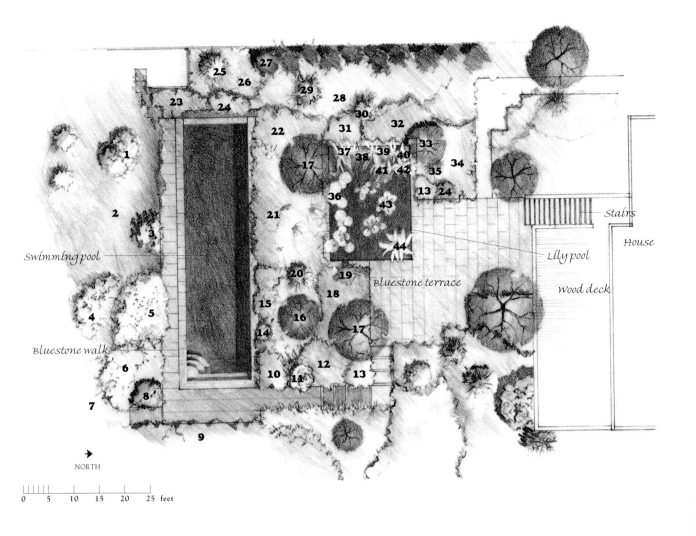

25
26
27
23
24
29
28
30
31
22
17
37 39
38
36
33
40
32
34
35
41 42
13 24
43
21
44
20
19
18
15
16
17
14
10
11
12
13

Swimming pool

Bluestone walk

Bluestone terrace

Lily pool

Stairs

House

Wood deck

1
2
3
4
5
6
7
8
9

→
NORTH

0   5   10   15   20   25 feet

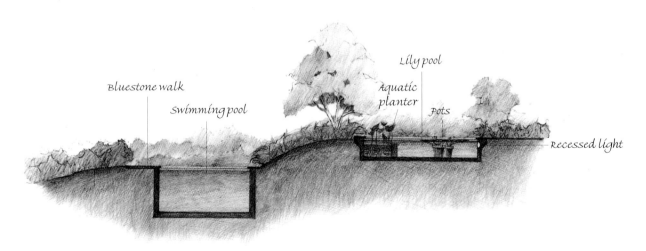

Bluestone walk

Swimming pool

Lily pool

Aquatic planter

Pots

Recessed light

shade the others. The surface of the beds is approximately eight inches below water level. He planted the tall *Thalia dealbata* in the corner bed next to the terrace, where it gives perspective to the whole pool. As a further accent, he planted *Myriophyllum aquaticum* at its base. Along the back of the pool, the large leaves of a long bed of *Nelumbo* spp. create a tropical feeling and obscure the edge. The beds at the end of the pool opposite the terrace contain a variety of plants, including *Pontederia cordata*, *Zizania latifolia*, and *Typha angustifolia*. The aquatics transition nicely to *Rudbeckia fulgida* 'Goldsturm' (black-eyed Susan) at the water's edge. Two water lilies occupy the center of the pool and are surrounded by *Nymphoides peltata*, which spreads inward from the edges.

In this garden, the proportions of the water surfaces and their relationships to each other and to the rest of the garden are especially important. Again, exaggerated size is the key to the garden's beauty. The lily pool is fifteen feet by twenty feet, almost as large as the adjacent sitting terrace, and the forty-six-foot-long swimming pool nearly spans the width of the garden.

Attracting wildlife is another good reason for having water in the garden. Wolfgang collects frogs, and friends know that he welcomes most unwanted fish and amphibians from their gardens. His animal friends seem especially at home in the summer, when the atmosphere of the garden becomes lush and tropical.

In the stillness of winter the leaves of
Thalia dealbata *hover like frosted*
sheets of tarnished silver over the
frozen lily pool.
Roger Foley photograph

The German-American Friendship Garden celebrates the three hundredth anniversary of the first German immigration to America. It was mandated by Congress and dedicated in 1988 by President Ronald Reagan and Chancellor Helmut Kohl.

The garden occupies a prestigious site on the National Mall in Washington, D.C. The Washington Monument rises just to the south and the White House faces the garden across the Ellipse to the north. I have been told that as many as seven million visitors walk this axis each year. Many find the garden a restful place to pause and reflect.

In addition to dazzling displays of plants native to both Germany and America, the garden features two "walk-in" fountains. The circular fountains' surfaces are flush with the surrounding pavement, defined

THE GERMAN-AMERICAN FRIENDSHIP GARDEN

only by a change of material to granite cobbles. The granite circles are "dished" for drainage. Each fountain has three columns of water, designed to erupt like geysers from the paving through flush bronze grates. The water falls directly back onto the grates and into underground reservoirs for recirculation. For safety reasons, it was important not to have standing water in such a public place.

The fountains attract people of all ages, especially during hot Washington summers. Some people walk right up to the water columns and touch them; others kick off their shoes and walk on the cool wet pavement; still others stop to rest on comfortable benches nearby. Children love it.

The design does not suffer from lack of water when the fountains are turned off in winter. Without water the granite surfaces simply become terraces, rather than unsightly and hazardous empty basins.

Rock Rim Ponds

THE CASTAGNA
REAL ESTATE COMPANY

R ock Rim Ponds is a 254-acre property in the historic countryside of Pound Ridge, New York. It is a scenic and ecological treasure of rugged topography, dense woodlands, and rock exposures surrounded by historic stone fences. Rolling meadow grasses sway in the breeze where farm crops once flourished, and dramatic natural displays of water erupt everywhere in the form of ponds, streams, and wetlands.

We have worked with this client for many years preparing and executing the plans for Rock Rim Ponds. The owner's objective is to enhance and protect, not alter, the inherent beauty and unique natural qualities of the land as he prepares it for residential development. This enlightened approach calls for only forty-eight homesites on the entire tract. Each site is nestled carefully amid a network of natural resources, scenic open spaces, wetland preserves, ponds, and streams. My design responsibilities include enhancing the natural water features that support this unconventional marketing approach. Indeed, water is the central theme and symbol of the entire development.

This project is about gardening with water on the broad scale of the residential community. The design approach I followed is similar to that I use for smaller projects; but the experi-

PRECEDING SPREAD & RIGHT: Pond edges, planted with grasses and aquatics in the spirit of a meadow, create a quietly romantic scene. Rocks placed strategically along the edge enhance the effect. A secret path encircles the pond through sophisticated but natural planting that hides the surrounding homesites.
RICHARD FELBER PHOTOGRAPHS

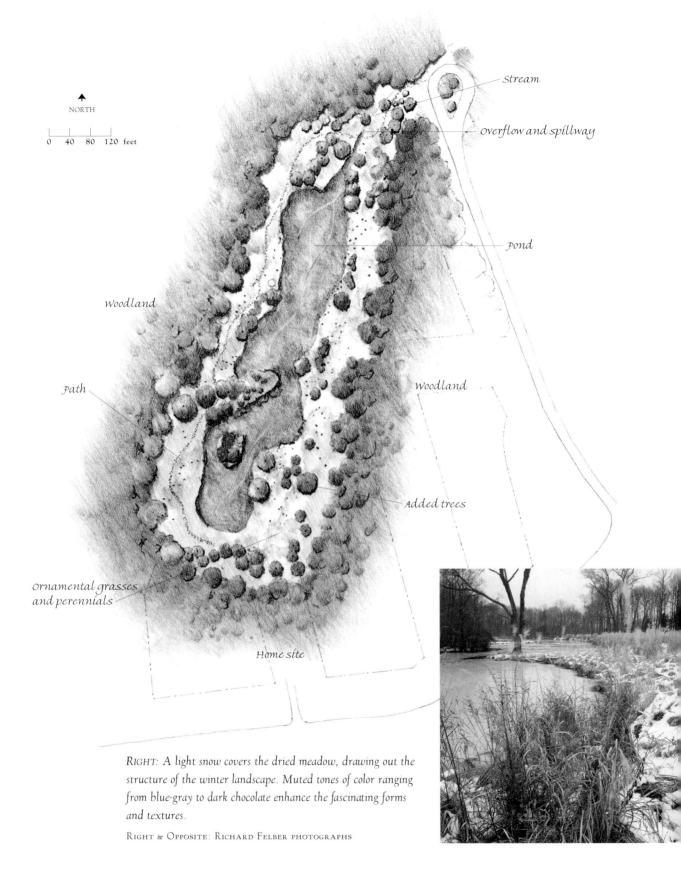

NORTH

0   40   80   120 feet

Stream

Overflow and spillway

Pond

Woodland

Woodland

Path

Added trees

Ornamental grasses
and perennials

Home site

RIGHT: *A light snow covers the dried meadow, drawing out the
structure of the winter landscape. Muted tones of color ranging
from blue-gray to dark chocolate enhance the fascinating forms
and textures.*

RIGHT & OPPOSITE: RICHARD FELBER PHOTOGRAPHS

ence greatly expanded my perception of water as a positive force in the residential environment. At Rock Rim Ponds I found myself planning water resources as habitats for wildlife, passive recreation for residents, and scenic vistas for neighboring homes. Practical uses such as drainage and erosion control were also crucial; the ponds even serve as reservoirs for irrigation and fire protection.

The design for the long and narrow pond seen here is representative of the total effort. Because of the excavation required to restore the pond's proper functioning, I was able to manipulate the shape of the new water surface. Notice how the edges change direction and how small peninsulas and islands interrupt views of the entire water surface. This simple visual trick leaves you wondering how far the water surface extends as it disappears around a bend. The result exaggerates our perceptions of scale, especially when the pond is seen from the homesites hidden on the ridge. Lesson: A little water goes a long way!

Planting and reforestation of the "necklace" around the pond where disturbance occurred during reclamation also has improved the water environment. Although the planting is sophisticated, it is also very natural. Native species in grand sweeps of color and texture merge with existing vegetation to control erosion and create wildlife habitats. A large meadow at one end of the pond displays grasses, perennials, and fruiting shrubs in every season. At the opposite end a shield of evergreens protects against the winter winds and provides shelter for birds. Wolfgang softened the edge of the water by planting reeds and other aquatics in selected areas and by placing boulders salvaged during excavation. In keeping with the spirit of a meadow, the planting is not weeded or maintained as a garden but allowed to develop naturally.

The pond reveals the obvious influence of Japanese design in its quiet simplicity, romantic delineation of edges, and placement of rocks. Residents can enjoy it close-up along a path that meanders along the entire perimeter. A treat along the way is a picturesque stone footbridge stretching over a weir. The spillway below is alternately a dry stream of beautiful rocks and a splashing rush of water into the forest beyond.

This hillside suburban property consists of two distinct garden environments. The upper level around the house is a very active place, where an energetic and growing family enjoys entertainment terraces, a swimming pool, a busy veranda, and a children's play lawn. The lower-level garden shown here is a found amenity—a leftover wooded space at the bottom of the slope, next to the borrowed scenery of a neighboring golf course. I used this space

TWIN BRIDGES

as a quiet retreat to complement the "hilltop" dynamics. It features a quiet walk along a natural woodland stream.

Stone steps and a sloping path arrive at the first of two footbridges that cross the stream. The stylized design of the wood bridges provides a bit of decorative interest and links the upper- and lower-level gardens. White balustrades are similar in detail to those on the veranda at the house. A clever detail incorporates benches on either side for sitting. Rambling trails, defined only by native stepping-stones dug into the surface, connect the bridges on either side of the stream. An edge of natural-looking boulders that seem to emerge naturally from the steeply sloping hillside controls the occasional rush of water during storms.

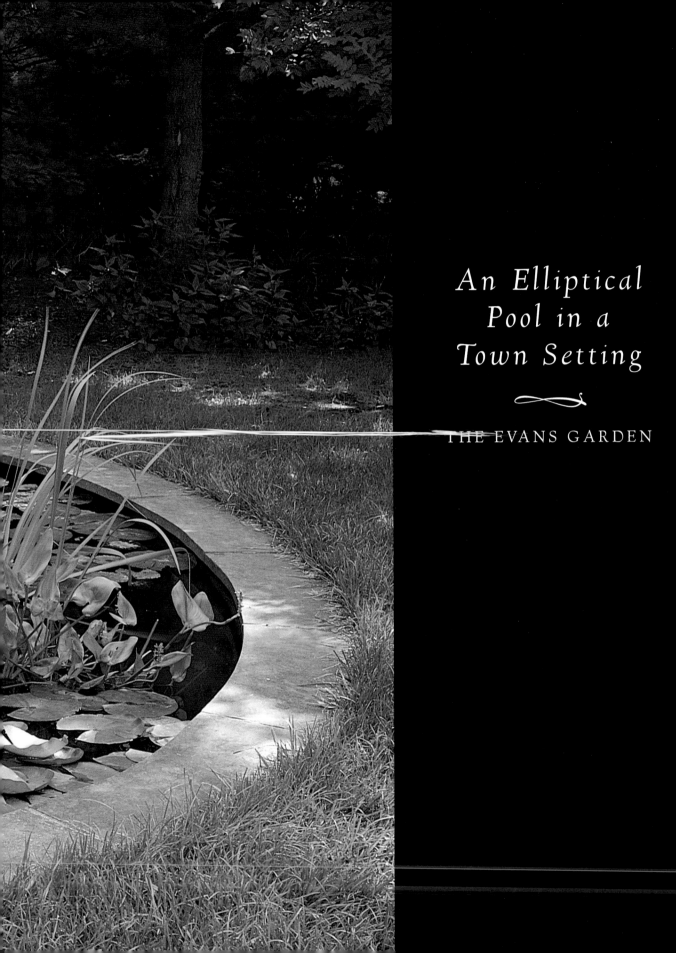

An Elliptical
Pool in a
Town Setting

THE EVANS GARDEN

This large elliptical lily pool anchors a very formal design for a small suburban garden. It focuses attention along a strong axis aligning the house, steps, and terrace. The long dimension of the ellipse falls directly on the axis, further stretching the linear effect of the garden.

A relaxed planting scheme provides the right measure of relief from the formal design. A dense border of planting next to the property line frames an open lawn. The pool seems to emerge naturally from the border planting and bridges the seam at the edge of the lawn. This is one of my favorite arrangements: a sharp edge of water on the near side of the pool gives way to a softer edge on the opposite side, where plants in the water and on the ground plane merge. The overall effect of the garden is orderly, yet lush and inviting.

Mary Evans is very sensitive to the ecology of the pool. Light, plants, and fish control the water quality, not chemicals. A balanced palette of water plants provides just the right amount of shade to control algae-activating sunlight. Her aim is to shade 75

percent of the pool. Floating *Eichhornia crassipes* (water hyacinth) shades the pool in the spring until the *Nymphaea* spp. and *Nelumbo* spp. bloom. Oxygenating plants, fish, and snails also contribute to the pristine quality of the water.

A single column of water rises from the center of the pool when Ms. Evans activates the fountain, and adds a festive accent to the garden scene. Since lilies prefer still water, she uses the fountain only intermittently—to entertain guests with its sounds and movement and to accompany her own quiet moments by the water's edge.

PRECEDING SPREAD: *The sharp edge of coping and lawn on one side of the pool gives way to soft planting on the other. The contrasting effect is orderly, yet lush and inviting.*
ABOVE & OPPOSITE: *A large elliptical lily pool, placed on axis with the house, steps, and terrace, is the centerpiece of this design. The resulting formality is softened by the relaxed planting design.*
OPPOSITE: JOHN NEUBAUER PHOTOGRAPH.

This garden was originally a level backyard behind a nondescript frame town house. Today it is an important part of a stunning indoor-outdoor living environment. Using a large L-shaped lily pool as a centerpiece, my primary goals for the transformation were to create three-dimensional interest and the illusion of more space.

To provide three-dimensional interest I lifted the surface of the pool behind a low wall. The wall is a comfortable sitting height and a favorite gathering place during parties. I also used the excess soil from the pool excavation to form a berm across the back of the garden. In addition to adding vertical relief, the berm gives additional height to the plants.

THE JERALD J. LITTLEFIELD GARDEN, VIRGINIA

To create the illusion of a larger space, I developed the indoor-outdoor aspects of the design, along with the size, shape, and placement of the pool. Seen through French doors from the dining room, the garden and pool become expanded parts of the downstairs living environment. The pool surface is relatively large; it takes up almost as much outdoor space as the terrace and planting areas. The length of the pool corresponds to the long dimension of the garden. This helps fool the mind into thinking this small urban space is deeper than it actually is. Finally, I placed the fountain jet on axis with the front door, creating a subtle tension that seems to pull the far edge of the pool into the line of vision as one enters the house.

JOHN NEUBAUER PHOTOGRAPH.

A Terrestrial
Sea on
Chesapeake Bay

THE CORBIN AND JEAN
GWALTNEY GARDEN

*T*he owner of this magnificent bayside estate graciously allows me to visit
often to photograph it or simply to show others what I consider to be a magical meeting of land and water. This garden is one of my favorite designs in a
natural water setting.

I often hear the word "breathtaking" when visitors first see this stunning view of
the Chesapeake Bay. Since the property is approached along a rural road that meanders
through field and woodland, the abrupt opening to the waterfront is a surprising visual
treat. I am delighted that most visitors' first reactions are followed by the understanding
that their eyes had been set up for the dramatic water view by the careful unfolding of
the foreground landscape.

To avoid competing with the natural grandeur of the site, the Gwaltneys settled on
a design approach for the "bones" of the garden that is restrained and disciplined. Its
main features are two great horizontal planes that step down from the house to the surface of the bay. Each is intended to resemble expanses of water.

The foreground plane is a broad wooden pool deck, detailed so that both the pool
and the deck surfaces appear to be on the same level. The pool is ultramarine blue,
which gives the illusion of great depth and adds to its reflective qualities. The proximity
of the pool to the bay creates the impression that the distance between the two is com-
pressed, that they are joined in some way, and that the water of the bay is pulled right

*Preceding Spread: A view from the house
in the spring shows great horizontal planes
of weathered cypress deck and expanses of
green lawn stepping down to the placid bay.
The understated design of the garden
allows the natural grandeur of the site to
shine through.*

*Left: Viewed from the house after a summer
rain, the visual effect of glistening deck and
ultramarine blue pool is to pull the bay
right up to the living space. Reflections of
the sky on the surface of the water draw light
and changing images into the center
of the garden.*

*Opposite: Reflections of dawn on a summer
morning include Calamagrostis acutiflora
stricta (feather reed grass), which anchors the
corner of the deck and blurs the edge of lawn
and bay.*

into the living space. The deck is simple and uncluttered. I notice
that the pool's surface reflects the sky and draws its light into the
garden, adding unexpected patterns of color and movement.

The second plane is a broad expanse of lawn, edged by a vast
border of perennial plantings. It is situated at an intermediate
level, four steps below the pool deck and seven feet above the surface of the bay at low mean tide. The lawn is flat and completely
unadorned except for the perennial edge and the majestic oaks that
rise abruptly and randomly from its surface. The lawn is intention-
ally reminiscent of water. I almost expect to see ripples around the
tree trunks, as if they had just pierced a placid lake of green.

The perennial border on the south, another major force in this
design, also symbolizes water. It has been planted as a great
"river," which emerges from the woods at the front of the house,
envelops the house and pool deck, turns toward the bay and
sweeps like a colorful "wetland marsh" along the edge of the great
lawn before finally emptying into the bay. The symbolic river
complements the overall theme and adds drama to this special
meeting place of land and water.

*RIGHT: Shown on a winter afternoon, stepping-stones lead
to the bay through a vast border of dried perennial plantings and majestic oaks. On the right, lit by the sun,
Miscanthus sinensis 'Giganteus' (giant silver grass)
keeps watch over the wintry scene.*

This extraordinary property is a peninsula jutting into the broad waters of the lower James River near Williamsburg, Virginia. The shape of the peninsula and level surface of the ground remind me of the deck of a ship. From the "bow" the river stretches out to the horizon on both sides and straight ahead.

I inherited the thoughtful master planning by Thomas Church and striking contemporary architecture when the owner asked me to extend the design into greater detail for construction. I quickly abandoned my standard bag of design tricks used to pull remote views of water into the living environment. This site already had water everywhere—up close and without boundaries. My job was to alleviate the sameness of the views. I designed view progressions, espe-

Dancing Point

cially by adding new elements of foreground interest; I framed views of more distant features; and, for balance, I even screened and blocked views in some places.

The planting design screens river views from the house through masses of perennials and ornamental grasses. I used the dock and dining gazebo to frame the view on one side of the house; an arbor designed as a folly draws attention to the foreground on the other. The design of the arbor was especially satisfying. I tied the house and arbor together visually by extending the exaggerated cornice detail of the dining room to this sculptural fantasy. The view is now across the garden from the dining room, through the stark columns of the arbor to the water and then on to the horizon.

Finally, notice how the sweeping horizontal planes of terraces and lawn mimic the river's surface and prepare the eye for the vast river panorama.

Pools and Cascade in a Ravine

THE JOHN AND SUSAN ULFELDER GARDEN

I think of this as a "teaching garden" because it brings so many design principles into play. Drama, surprise, contrast, sound, borrowed scenery, and visual trickery enhance the water theme. These lessons and other design "secrets" are part of this garden tour.

The backdrop is a wooded ravine, protected in the public interest as a part of the Potomac River watershed in northern Virginia. Neighboring houses are hidden by the dense forest, and artificial boundaries, such as hedgerows or fences, are invisible. The approach to the Ulfelder house is from above, along a steep and picturesque roadway that is little more than an enhanced woodland trail. The road ends as a sweeping circle of granite cobbles in front of the house.

In simplest terms, the design consists of a small lily pool on the upper level, a swimming pool some fourteen feet below, and a connecting path of stepping-stones arranged as a "dry cascade." The lily pool initiates an illusory rush of water down the rocky "stream" to the swimming pool. This simple design approach has a powerful effect.

Many first-time visitors hesitate before knocking at the front door because they want first to investigate the unmistakable sound of gently splashing water. The source is the small lily pool and waterfall nestled next to the drive. It is a subtle introduction in a progressive drama of water "events." Aquatic plants on either side of the small pool define an open channel and lead the eye from the waterfall, across the pool, to the dry-cascade path of stone steps. The steeply descending stairs disappear quickly around the corner of the house where the visitor comes upon an unexpected scene: the horizontal plane of a large swimming pool and its terrace appear suspended at the edge of a wooded

PRECEDING SPREAD: The swimming pool and terrace appear suspended at the edge of the wooded ravine. The pool seems ready to spill over its sinuous edge into the woods. The reflection of the forest adds drama and depth to the scene.

RIGHT & OPPOSITE: Visitors trace the sound of gently splashing water to a lily pool nestled between the circular entrance drive, front porch, and stone retaining wall. Aquatic plants on either side of the pool define an open channel that leads the eye first to a dry cascade of stone steps and then to the swimming pool on the terrace below.

ROGER FOLEY PHOTOGRAPHS

ravine. The brimming pool seems ready to spill into the woods at any moment. The opposite side of the ravine is forested and adds to the drama as it rises far above the pool level.

The swimming pool and terrace are dramatic angular forms amid natural surroundings. From the house, one can see the dark waters of the pool reflect wonderful images of the forest and changing sky. It reminds me of a quiet lagoon at the edge of a forest. The swimming pool is key to the soft transition between built and natural environments. The pool's straight edges on the near side anchor it to the architecture of the house, while its sensuous curve on the far side leads the eye to the spectacular view of undisturbed nature.

The details of the hardscape design are like final brushstrokes on a painting. Notice especially how the dry stream appears to "pool" as it penetrates the otherwise geometric pattern of the terrace. Note also the contrasting edge patterns in the paving, the mitered corners of the pool coping, and pool steps that make you want to step right in.

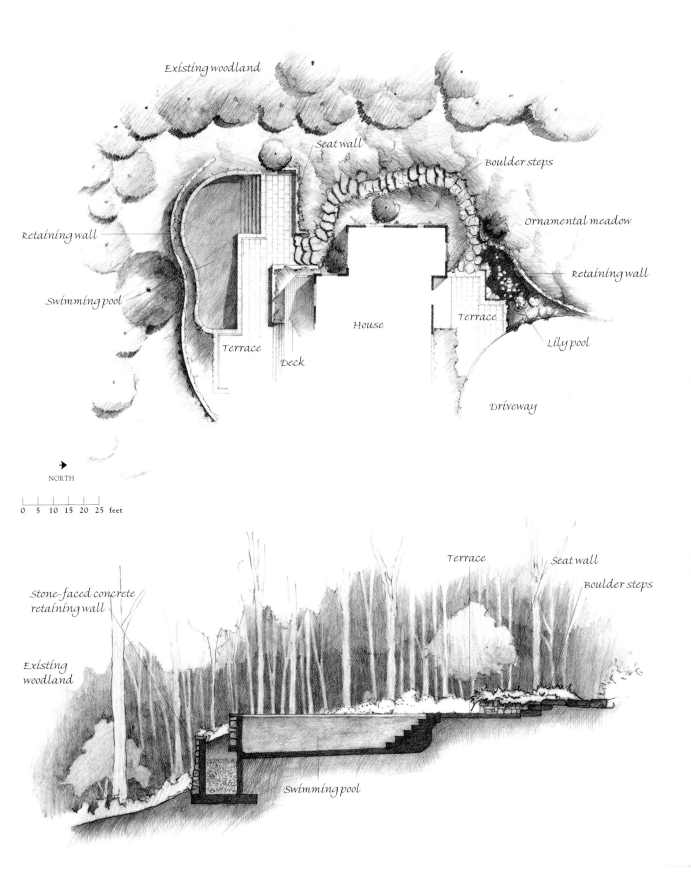

Existing woodland

Seat wall

Boulder steps

Ornamental meadow

Retaining wall

Retaining wall

Swimming pool

House

Terrace

Lily pool

Terrace

Deck

Driveway

NORTH

0 5 10 15 20 25 feet

Terrace

Seat wall

Boulder steps

Stone-faced concrete
retaining wall

Existing
woodland

Swimming pool

S tarting with sound but undistinguished architecture and few site amenities, I worked with the Hamowys to personalize their weekend retreat on Long Island. We agreed to construct a large lily pool opposite the entrance terrace as the site's new centerpiece. "Large," in this case, means twenty by thirty-six feet! The pool's size makes a dramatic statement at the very entrance to the house.

THE MR. AND MRS. EDWIN HAMOWY GARDEN

Visitors don't see the pool when they first arrive at the circular driveway; it is hidden behind low garden walls and only emerges as an eye-popping surprise when one steps up to the entrance terrace. Once inside the house, guests become aware that the pool is much more than an entry feature; it is a center of attention throughout the house. The living-room space, for example, seems to overflow through broad glass doors directly onto the pool surface. Subtle activity produced by a single jet of water in the pool directly opposite the glass doors heightens this effect. A backdrop of lush foliage emerges from the pool and garden behind it. Mysterious reflections in the dark water and on the living-room ceiling complete the dramatic indoor-outdoor composition.

A pool is often appropriately sited at the front of a house when the back is too shady or too small or when a gardener simply wants to delight guests with a gesture of welcome and whimsy. Water adds great life and sparkle to any entrance.

Wolfgang designed this small pool to act as an element of surprise next to the Adlers' front door. The pool is hidden behind low

THE MR. AND MRS. ABRAHAM L. ADLER GARDEN

retaining walls that create a slightly elevated pedestal for the house. One discovers it by walking up three broad steps to the entrance stoop. It fills the moment just before entering the house with reflective images and the quiet sounds of moving water.

The pool is very modest in size, but its design is sophisticated. The natural stone edge is compatible with the rustic wood and stone pier construction of the house. Water plantings obscure its far edge and blend naturally with plantings on the ground plane beyond. Overhanging boulders placed randomly around the edge add greater dimension to the water surface. A simple garden faucet, operated manually, provides recharge and the occasional music of rushing water.

JONATHAN BLAIR PHOTOGRAPH.

Waterfall
and Pool in the
Capital City

PENNSYLVANIA AVENUE
DEVELOPMENT
CORPORATION

*P*ennsylvania Avenue from the U.S. Capitol to the White House in Washington, D.C., is the site of a decades-long revitalization effort. Today, as "America's Main Street," it is a magnificent boulevard and worthy host to inaugural parades and other national celebrations. It has been my privilege for many years to participate directly in its transformation by redesigning and supervising seasonal maintenance of all the streetscape plantings on the avenue from the U.S. Treasury to the National Gallery.

Pershing Park is nestled at the western end of the avenue. It is a powerful example of water's positive effect on the urban environment. Conceived originally by M. Paul Friedberg, landscape architect, the park is an ingenious three-dimensional composition. Visitors descend broad granite steps from street level and surrounding berms to a secluded, almost hidden, oasis of splashing water and lush plantings. The hypnotic sights and sounds of water cascading over the walls of a great granite box onto steps and into an oversized pool are in startling contrast to the bustle of the city, just steps away.

Our collaboration with Mr. Friedberg on the park design grew out of our responsibilities for planting the rest of the avenue. Our objectives were to soften the hard edges of this highly structured waterside space and to cool it down, especially during Washington's hot summers. The planting areas are very small, consisting mostly of planter boxes embedded in the stairs and around the pool. Wolfgang chose a very simple plant palette and used it on an overstated and dramatic scale. He filled the planter boxes to overflowing and encouraged foliage to cascade over adjacent steps, pavement, and water. The resulting profusion feels tropical; it resembles a small botanic garden with much shade, seasonal interest, and color. The steps are now a favorite sitting place in summer for sightseers and workers to enjoy the cooling effects of shade and water.

For eight years we tried to convince the client that planting the pool with aquatics was necessary to

PRECEDING SPREAD: At the far side of the large pool, water cascades over the sides of a gigantic granite box. The sounds of falling water mask noises of busy city streets just a few steps away.

Broad granite steps and surrounding berms hide this oasis of lush plantings where visitors discover a resting place with shade and water. The foliage resembles a mini–botanic garden as it cascades in great masses over steps and pavement into the water. The summer effect is tropical, but seasonal interest and color continue year-round. VOLKMAR K. WENTZEL PHOTOGRAPH

OPPOSITE: The translucent leaves, brilliant red stems, and spidery flowers of Thalia geniculata rubra *(red-stemmed water canna) are like stained glass, back-lit here by the sun. Salmon-colored flowers of* Canna glauca 'Erebus' *(water canna) glow in the distance.*
BELOW: In winter, the National Park Service moves the water plants to aquatic greenhouses and the pool is transformed into a popular ice skating rink.
JOHN NEUBAUER PHOTOGRAPH

complete the park. At last we succeeded, and we then extended the lushness of the overall planting scheme by choosing large-leaved plants for the pool: *Thalia geniculata rubra* (red-stemmed water canna), *Canna glauca* 'Erebus' (salmon-pink water canna), *Nelumbo* spp., and *Nymphaea* spp. The water plants are rotated in and out of the pool on a seasonal basis.

The public responded enthusiastically to the water plantings and some unexpected visitors were also pleased. Immediately after we planted in the water, habitat-starved ducks moved in and added a lively new dimension to the design. Visitors enjoy them and forgive their occasional eating of the foliage for salad.

I pass Pershing Park often and notice its attractions year-round, not just in summer. Spring is celebrated in a blaze of flowering bulbs. Autumn changes the foliage, bleaches the grasses, and creates a pointillist effect in the form of dried seed heads. And in winter the pool is especially active as a popular skating rink.

The Bennett/ Born Garden

The focus of this elaborate town garden is a combination lily pool and fountain set against the back wall of the site. Positioned like a small stage behind a broad terrace, the pool and fountain provide a compelling water show from all vantage points. The animated water scene creates an indoor attraction as well, because it can be seen through windows and glass doors at the back of the house.

The fountain's merit is its simplicity. A bronze shell is attached to the wall about four feet above the surface of the pool. Recirculated water from the pool fills the shell through plumbing concealed in the wall. Trickles of water overflow the scalloped edge of the shell into the pool. Splashing water decorates the brick wall and sends concentric ripples across the pool surface. Occasional breezes alter the pattern of falling water.

This tiny town garden was originally designed by Hugh Newell Jacobsen and Lester Collins. When I was invited to study the garden, a canal across the back third of the space had fallen into disrepair, but interesting elements of the garden remained: a low retaining wall that defined a raised planting bed between the pool and the back garden wall, and a bluestone terrace that filled most of the foreground.

Having a ready source of water made it easy to enhance the garden. I used part of the planting bed at the rear of the space to create a raised basin. Water pumped from the pool fills the basin, overflows a lip on the front edge, and returns to the pool as a cascade over the face of the wall. This simple operation brings the water to life. The elevated surface of water in the basin enhances the garden's three-dimensional qualities and draws attention to the original pool. In addition, the waterfall brings needed aeration to the water and masks the occasional noise of planes taking off from and landing at a nearby airport.

THE PAUL L. HOUTS, JAN MUNHALL-HOUTS GARDEN

Waterfall
in the Woods

THE SHOCKEY GARDEN

*T*he Shockeys' house lies at the end of a farm road that winds through dense woods. The first time I drove in, I was unprepared for the sight of the immense white concrete house set in a clearing on the hillside. Its distinctive contemporary design (a showplace for Mr. Shockey's concrete-products business) contrasted sharply with the surrounding forest.

The house had just been completed, and the Shockeys had moved in, but no landscaping or site improvements had begun. Each of the building's four floors was anchored firmly into what appeared to be a mud bank, the result of clearing and construction work, done with heavy equipment, on the site's steep slope. The Shockeys understandably felt apprehensive—even desperate—about the condition of the property. I was delighted to accept their challenge.

Although there are no natural sources of water here, such as a stream or spring, right away I imagined using water to connect the stark, man-made structure to its densely forested site. I conceived an image of rocky outcroppings and cascading water splashing from pool to pool, finding its way from the upper level near the entrance court to an outdoor living and entertainment terrace some twenty-two feet below. Admittedly, my image was inspired by Falling Water, the masterly marriage of nature and building by Frank Lloyd Wright at Bear Run, Pennsylvania.

Unlike the natural cascading stream that flows beneath Falling Water, the waterfall that I realized at Shockeys is all theater, built from scratch and operated by pumps. Even the series of rocky rivulets that emerges from the woods above the house and finally disappears into the woods below is a watery illusion, achieved by placing rocks randomly "upstream" and "downstream" in the Japanese "dry stream" tradition.

PRECEDING SPREAD: *Water begins its descent at the entrance court, then cascades over four waterfalls before reaching the large pool at the garden terrace below. The sound of water rushing over Stoneyhurst flagging (a local stone) provides a cooling interlude of music. The stones are a pleasing contrast to the clean white concrete walls of the house.*
ROGER FOLEY PHOTOGRAPH

ABOVE: *Reflections of sky and trees greet visitors at the entrance court of the Shockey residence. This upper-level pool is like a pond in a continuous brook that spills abruptly over the narrow ledge shown in the distance. Beyond the spill is a waterfall event that ends some twenty-two feet below.*

OPPOSITE: ROGER FOLEY PHOTOGRAPH

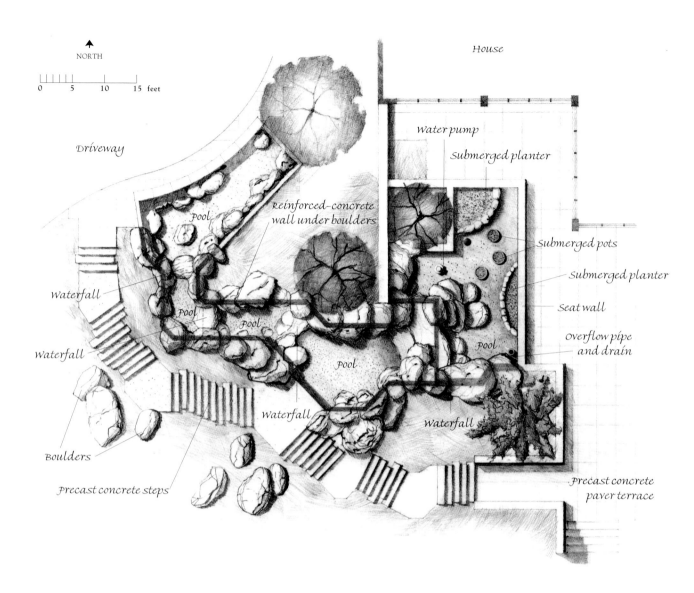

NORTH

0 5 10 15 feet

Driveway

House

Water pump

Submerged planter

Reinforced-concrete
wall under boulders

Pool

Submerged pots

Submerged planter

Seat wall

Waterfall

Pool

Pool

Overflow pipe
and drain

Waterfall

Pool

Pool

Waterfall

Boulders

Waterfall

Precast concrete steps

Precast concrete
paver terrace

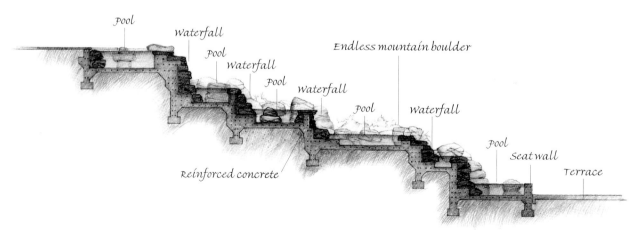

Pool

Waterfall

Pool

Waterfall

Pool

Endless mountain boulder

waterfall

Pool

waterfall

Pool

Seat wall

Reinforced concrete

Terrace

The upper-level pool, which first can be seen from the entrance drive, reinforces the image of a continuous brook, which ponds briefly at the waterfall, then rushes on. The twenty-foot vertical "theater" includes a sequence of water events, including four spills into five pools, each placed carefully to maximize visual and sound effects, and a parallel system of broad steps and landings that appears to tumble in alternating directions beside the waterfall. The steps allow comfortable movement from one level to the next and encourage visitors to explore ponds and plants along the way.

The sound of water falling from several heights into multiple pools provides an unexpected bit of musical magic. The quality, pitch, and rhythm of sound that each waterfall makes is unique, depending on the dimensions, the quantity of water flowing,

and the depth of pool. Heard altogether, the sounds converge to become a liquid symphony as one moves from place to place in the garden.

The pool at the garden's lowest level is the largest and is heavily planted and stocked with fish. Its surface is bench height above the terrace floor and the pool's edge is a seat wall. I have observed that people are drawn to this edge, where they can sit close to the water. The image of party guests happily dipping their hands in the water, waiting to be nuzzled by the fish, symbolizes water's mysterious attraction. It is also a satisfying indication of a successful design.
ROGER FOLEY PHOTOGRAPH.

PRECEDING PAGE: Cascading water splashes from pool to pool over rocky outcroppings on its way to the terrace level.
ROGER FOLEY PHOTOGRAPH.

The beautiful reflecting pool shown here is a swimming pool in disguise. As the centerpiece of a stunning town garden, the pool serves this garden in two ways: as a lap pool for swimming in the summer and as a mirror for the exquisite surroundings throughout the year. Lester Collins designed the original garden and Hugh Newell Jacobsen designed the pool. My role came later when I was asked to enhance the poolside planting, which can now be seen reflected on the surface of the water.

The original placement of the long pool on axis with the living-room windows established a very formal look. A design trick exaggerates the linear effect: as seen from the house, the pool appears to be elongated because the near width (eight feet) is greater than the distant width (seven feet). Also, the lamp-black tint of the final parget coat on the pool wall deepens the mysterious reflective qualities of the water and blurs the distinction between pool surface and surrounding blue-stone terrace.

A magnificent stand of *Phyllostachys aureosulcata* (yellow-groove bamboo) flanks one side of the pool. The rustling sounds and swaying movements entertain in all seasons. Under the weight of summer rains and winter snows the canes arch over the pool and garden like a protective shell. A stainless-steel root barrier sunk two and a half feet in the ground controls the invasive roots of the bamboo.

JOHN NEUBAUER PHOTOGRAPH

Only a garden of great elegance and scale could match the casual splendor of this carefully restored "arts and crafts" house. This distinctive American style, popular at the turn of the century, was my inspiration for the design of the garden. The house is positioned perfectly for lofty garden views from many rooms, balconies, terraces, doors, and stairways.

I chose a lower level space at the back of the house for a large lily pool and terrace garden. The pool is circular, sixteen feet in diameter. A wide cobble terrace and stone retaining walls, capped with bluestone at sitting height, ring the pool. The radial pattern of cobbles on the terrace floor leads the eye to the center of the pool, where a single jet of water erupts in a subtle show of sound and motion.

THE SIMON AND ROSITA TRINCA GARDEN

An elaborate border of planting, designed in the spirit of a "cottage garden," embraces three quadrants of the circular terrace; the remaining quarter-circle of steps moves up to a large dining terrace.

A rich palette of natural materials—granite cobbles, brick, gravel, and bluestone—contributes to the relaxed atmosphere of the garden. One sees many of these interesting surface materials at the pool terrace, since it is the arrival place for paths and walkways. A primary path connects the lily pool and the swimming pool, which is removed in its own world behind a lacy curtain of *Betula nigra* (river birch).

RICHARD FELBER PHOTOGRAPH

Paradise Manor is an urban neighborhood of more than six hundred garden apartments in northeast Washington, D.C. The project had suffered from years of neglect and deterioration when I was invited to collaborate with the owner and a team of specialists to comprehensively redesign and renovate the project. Our goal, now successfully completed, was to reestablish a safe, supportive, and attractive residential environment.

We proposed the site of the neighborhood's activities to be an outdoor court: a social and recreational gathering place for residents of all ages. The centerpiece of the park is a combination sculpture fountain and water play area. Three spirited dolphins, sculpted of smooth reinforced concrete, sit on the

PARADISE MANOR

coping of a shallow pool. During summer months the dolphins spit jets of water into the pool and onto neighborhood children who come to enjoy the cooling spray. The design reminds me of lawn sprinklers my mother set out for me to run through when I was a child. Simple, but great fun in the hot summer!

The magic of the fountain lies in its simplicity. The water system is not elaborate or sophisticated. Residents simply turn it on during the summer when children are most likely to enjoy it. For safety purposes the pool is a shallow bowl with a drain in the bottom so the water does not collect. Since water flows directly from the tap and drains away immediately, treating it is unnecessary, unlike the case of a wading or swimming pool.

As sculpture, the dolphin fountain adds enduring pleasure: it is a beautiful neighborhood attraction with or without water and throughout the year.

A Hilltop Lily Pool with Waterfall

THE JERALD J.
LITTLEFIELD GARDEN,
MARYLAND

The design for this garden came to me on my first visit to the site. The house was still under construction, and a huge pile of rocks, the spoils of the basement's excavation, dominated the backyard. I had never seen this kind of stone before in the Washington area. I later learned that it is iron oxide quartz and that it is reputed to contain gold. The color is a beautiful red-orange. Blasting for excavation had created random boulder shapes that might work as landscape features. Dr. Littlefield agreed immediately that the rocks should not be removed from the site but used instead to create a "natural spring" with a waterfall and pool as the garden's centerpiece. A swimming pool of generous dimensions would complete the waterscape.

I considered the size and placement of the lily pool first. The site I chose for the pool is seen from a "great room" on the main level of the house and from windows and small

decks upstairs. Views of the pool from above are especially interesting. I was careful to center the pool on axis with the imposing fireplace on the far wall of the great room. The visual axis that connects fireplace to pool reinforces the indoor-outdoor atmosphere and adds to a sense of spaciousness.

The design for the lily pool easily fell into place. Rocks from our "found" collection emerge as natural outcroppings from an earth berm on the far side of the pool. A small "spring" and waterfall, which emerge from among rocks nestled into the berm, feed the primary basin with recirculated water. The surface

PRECEDING SPREAD: A small "spring" and waterfall emerge from a rocky earth berm at the far side of the pool. A bench-height wall contains the pool on the near side and provides a resting place next to the cooling water and colorful fish.
LEFT & OPPOSITE: Water ripples over beautiful red-orange stones that were found during excavation and placed to resemble natural outcroppings.

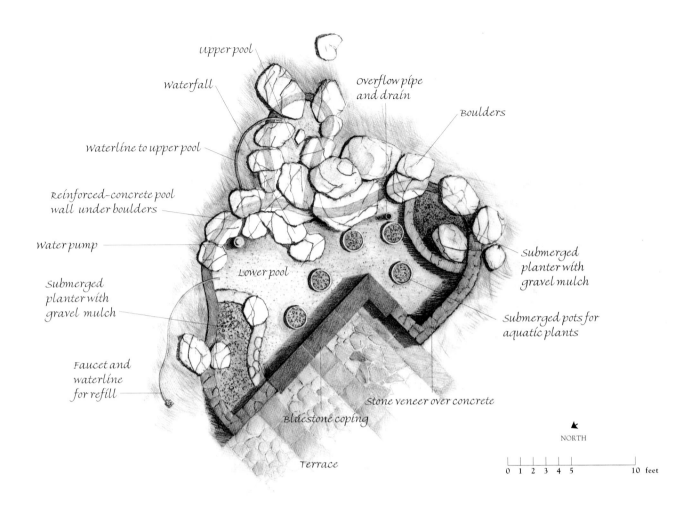

upper pool

Waterfall

Overflow pipe
and drain

Boulders

Waterline to upper pool

Reinforced-concrete pool
wall under boulders

Water pump

Lower pool

Submerged
planter with
gravel mulch

Submerged
planter with
gravel mulch

Submerged pots for
aquatic plants

Faucet and
waterline
for refill

Stone veneer over concrete

Bluestone coping

Terrace

NORTH

0 1 2 3 4 5   10 feet

Spotlight

Waterfall

Boulders

Bluestone
coping

Recessed light

Terrace

Water lily in submerged pot

Concrete basin
for upper pool

Reinforced-concrete
pool wall

AQUATIC PLANTS

1. TYPHA MINIMA
2. MYRIOPHYLLUM AQUATICUM
3. THALIA DEALBATA
4. ACORUS CALAMUS 'VARIEGATUS'
5. NYMPHAEA SPP.
6. NELUMBO NUCIFERA
   East Indian Lotus
7. LYTHRUM SALICARIA
   Loosestrife
8. IRIS PSEUDACORUS
9. DULCHIUM ARUNDINACEUM

GARDEN PLANTS

10. HEUCHERA X 'BRESSINGHAM HYBRIDS'
    Coral Bells
11. ECHINACEA PURPUREA
    Purple Coneflower
    with
    LIATRIS SPICATA
    Gay feather
12. FARGESIA NITIDA
    Clump Bamboo

13. ASTER FRIKARTII 'MOENCH'
    Hardy Purple aster
14. HOSTA X 'HONEYBELLS'
    Plantain Lily
15. IRIS SIBIRICA 'CAESAR'S BROTHER'
16. HYPERICUM X 'HIDCOTE'
    St. John's Wort
17. HYPERICUM CALYCINUM 'SUNGOLD'
    St. John's Wort
18. MOLINEA ARUNDINACEA 'WINDSPIEL'
    Tall Purple Moor Grass
    with
    BRUNNERA MACROPHYLLA
    Dwarf Anchusa

Upper pool

Waterfall

Lower pool

Coping

Terrace

NORTH

0 1 2 3 4 5   10 feet

A HILLTOP LILY POOL WITH WATERFALL   145

of the pool is raised like a stage above the terrace, impounded by a stone sitting wall. The pool's crisp edge along the sitting wall contrasts with the soft plantings and rocky outcroppings that obscure the pool's edge on the opposite side.

I designed the terrace to be an extension of the pool environment. After it rains, when water is trapped briefly in mortar joints, the terrace becomes a sparkling fluid plane. At night, cove lights, hidden beneath the bench on the sitting wall, bathe its smooth surface.

The swimming pool inhabits its own world behind a scrim of *Betula nigra* (river birch), and completes the garden composition. The forty-foot by ten-foot surface of the pool provides a visual "landing" from which other horizontal planes, such as the porch, lily pool, and terraces gradually ascend through the garden. The subtle variations in elevation from surface to surface create an intriguing illusion of expansiveness in this small garden.

PART III

BUILD

A 20-mil vinyl liner is being placed on a newly
excavated "farm pond." The pond shell is
sculpted to provide underwater shelves for planting. The liner will be covered with twelve inches
of soil for stability and damage protection.

ISSUES

Site Preparation and Excavation

Once you have chosen the location for your lily pool or fountain and you have the required building permits in hand, you can begin to build. The first step is to lay out the pool on the ground with stakes and string or a garden hose. At this point it's always fun to refine the shape, fine-tune the location, and make other minor adjustments in the design.

Before you start to dig, decide how deep your pool will be. I take several factors into account at this point. In general, the deeper the pool, the more expensive it will be to construct and maintain. Deep pools require more excavation, are more difficult to plant, and require more water and maintenance. Often the most important reason to limit the depth to twenty-four inches is that in most jurisdictions a deeper pool will qualify as a swimming pool, requiring a fence, self-closing gates, and depth markers. I consider the optimum depth to be from eighteen inches to twenty-four inches in order to sustain an adequate temperature and depth for fish and plants.

When actually digging a pool, I always excavate into the existing grade. If the shell is built on fill, it will settle and possibly crack. In this case you may have to drive concrete piles into the earth to the original grade, which in effect means building on columns. I would recommend consulting with a structural engineer to be sure the detailing is correct. Finally, water is always level, of course, and the slightest error will make the pool look tilted. It is very important that the basin rim be perfectly level. I do this by simply setting a two-by-four across the shell and checking it using a hand level.

Pool Types

There are many materials available for the shell of your pool. I usually use a concrete shell and, rarely, a vinyl liner. You have seen examples of both in Part II, "Design." In the Jacobs Garden, concrete is used for the shell of the pool (page 38). You can also buy a fiberglass basin from your local nursery.

LEFT: *Gunite is being "shot" from a hose to form this pool shell. The wood forms are required only to define the top edge of the pool; otherwise, the excavation itself acts as the form. The reinforcing bars placed to prevent the basin from cracking are clearly visible.*
OPPOSITE: *The wall of the lily pool in the Simon and Rosita Trinca Garden is formed in wood and ready to receive concrete.*

Polyvinyl chloride (PVC) and Butyl rubber are flexible materials that are easy to install in both large farm ponds and standard lily pools. They are cheaper than concrete and easier to construct, but they are more prone to be punctured by tools, the sharp claws of a raccoon fishing at night, or even by the new shoots of plants along the edge. Both are available in large sheets and rolls and can be joined with liner sealing tape and repaired with liner patching tape. A Butyl liner is more durable than the PVC and twice as expensive.

POOL LINER WITH PLANTER & BOULDER

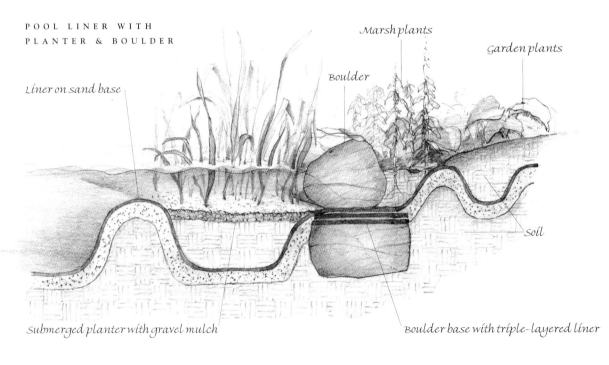

Marsh plants

Garden plants

Boulder

Liner on sand base

Soil

Submerged planter with gravel mulch

Boulder base with triple-layered liner

When I use a vinyl liner, I am very careful to disguise the rim for esthetic reasons. I do this in several ways: by planting at the water's edge; creating planters underwater by forming a "dish" in the soil; placing rocks on underwater shelves that are cut into the slope at varying elevations on the bottom (see detail, opposite); and by cantilevering terraces over the water a few inches to create crisp shadows and cleverly conceal the liner beneath (see detail, below). When I build a large pond, I line the basin with a twelve-inch layer of clay on top of the liner.

I prefer to use concrete, Gunite, or shotcrete for the pool shell. They are durable and can be formed into any shape or size. But they are more expensive and difficult to construct than PVC or Butyl rubber liners, and there is no room for error because once installed, they are very difficult to change. Both require reinforcing bars placed vertically and horizontally at twelve-inch intervals. The bars prevent the basin from cracking (see photo, opposite).

A concrete shell requires that you build a wood form in order to hold its shape when it is poured (see photo below). I pour a concrete shell in two stages: the floor first and the walls second. To prevent the seam between floor and walls from leaking, I use a "water stop" made of a continuous rubber strip embedded in the concrete at the seam (see detail, page 154). Pouring concrete requires that the truck have good access to the job site in order to get close enough to the pool to pour; otherwise the concrete will have to be moved by hand in a wheelbarrow.

LINER WITH STONE COPING

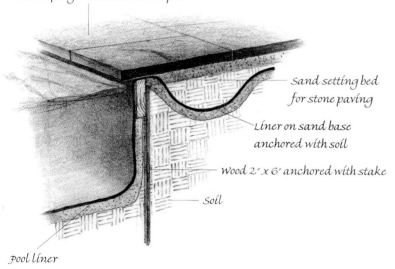

Stone coping cantilevered over pool

sand setting bed
for stone paving

Liner on sand base
anchored with soil

Wood 2″ x 6″ anchored with stake

Soil

Pool liner

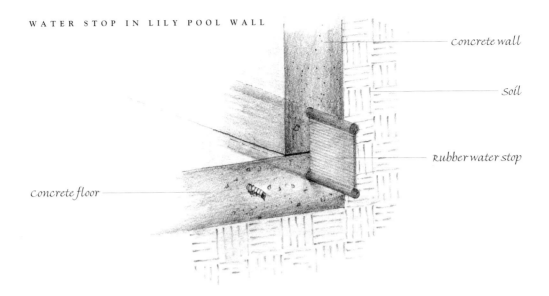

concrete wall

soil

rubber water stop

concrete floor

Gunite and shotcrete are trade names for concrete that is mixed with air under high pressure and "shot" through a hose to form the pool shell. Wood forms are used only to define the edge. The excavation itself acts as the form (see photograph, page 152). Accessibility is less important with this method, since the hose can be up to two hundred feet long.

When the concrete, Gunite, or shotcrete is in place I let it cure for at least seven days, after which it is plastered with portland cement and allowed to dry thoroughly. Then all surfaces are cleaned with diluted muriatic acid and painted with pool epoxy, which is available at any aquatic nursery (see photograph, below). I prefer to use black

LEFT: The Jacobses' lily pool is ready to be filled with water. All surfaces are clean and the shell has been painted with black pool epoxy.

OPPSITE TOP: A grid of PVC pipe, designed for the safety of children, is supported at the edges of this lily pool. It can be lifted easily from the pool for cleaning. The grid dimensions are large enough for aquatic plants to grow through but small enough to protect fish from common predators.

OPPOSITE BOTTOM: A rubber water stop, placed between the concrete beam and cobble coping of the Simon and Rosita Trinca Garden, allowed me to raise the water level almost to the top of the coping.

epoxy because it makes the pool look natural, deep, and mysterious. Fish will stand out clearly. Before I fill the pool with water, I let the paint dry. I flush it out once with water, then fill it again and plant it. I let it stand for four weeks and then check the pH (for the degree of acidity). It should be in the neutral range of about seven. This will ensure that the fish will survive when they are put in the water.

If you decide to use a fiberglass pool, remember that it is preformed and rigid. I find the sizes and shapes of manufactured liners too limiting for my gardens. They are useful if you want a quick, simple lily pool because, like the ubiquitous washtub, they are easy to install, require no maintenance, and will last a lifetime. The small size may be just the thing for your garden, especially if the space is small. Because they will support themselves, they can be used above ground sitting on a terrace or lawn. You should consider how to transport the liners, because fiberglass pools generally are manufactured in one piece.

WATER STOP WITH COBBLE COPING

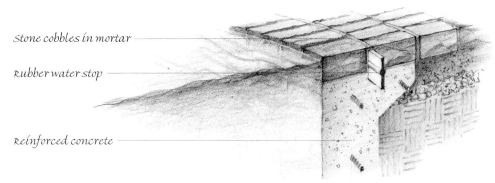

Stone cobbles in mortar

Rubber water stop

Reinforced concrete

Coping / Edging

I use various types of edging and coping, depending on the type of pool I've designed and the desired effect. The straight lines and precise dimensions of manufactured materials, such as brick, limestone, and precast concrete, create a formal look; native stone and other materials are better for a more natural look. Pool coping often plays a functional role as well. For example, it may hold the perimeter of a flexible liner in place and protect exposed edges from damaging ultraviolet rays. Coping may also be designed as a sitting wall, a base for sculpture and plant containers, or a cove for lighting (see the Littlefield Garden on page 140).

Since pool edges and coping are so visible, their detailing and craftsmanship are very important. For example, when using a material of uniform thickness such as brick or bluestone, it is important to keep the coping absolutely level. The eye tends to follow the waterline under the coping and detects sags and slopes, however slight. Also, I set the bottom edge of the coping as close as possible to the water level, an inch or less above it if possible, and let the coping overhang the water by at least two inches (see detail, below). Many materials are available for copings. Pennsylvania bluestone is one of my favorites. I specify at least a two-inch thickness for all pieces, and they must be uniformly thick. Stones that are too thin will appear weak and flimsy and stones of varying thickness look sloppy. Other masonry materials that I use include brick and precast concrete (see the garden on page 72 and the Shockey Garden on page 128). Since both are manufactured materials, their thickness is uniform.

BRICK POOL COPING

Brick coping

Reinforced concrete

Soil

A carefully articulated pattern of
Pennsylvania bluestone adds a highly finished look to the pool coping and terrace
in the John and Susan Ulfelder Garden.
ROGER FOLEY PHOTOGRAPH

I often use stones and boulders at the edge of a pool to create or enhance a natural look (see the Hester Garden on page 66). Stones should be placed either completely inside or outside the pool and not intersect the wall of the basin (see photograph, left). Joints between boulders and concrete will crack and leakage will occur because of differing effects of thermal expansion and contraction.

Wood also can be used at a pool's edge. A cantilevered wood deck or bridge gives a dramatic effect. Remember to specify decay-resistant woods, such as redwood or cedar, or woods treated with chemical preservatives. But bear in mind that redwood that is not fully aged and woods treated with creosote or arsenic are toxic to fish.

LILY-POOL WALL
WITH STONE FACING

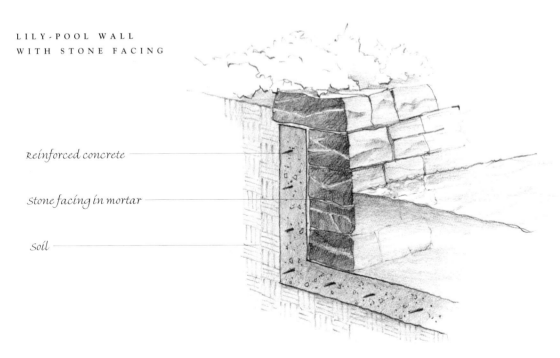

Reinforced concrete

Stone facing in mortar

Soil

INVISIBLE EDGE OF CONCRETE
POOL WALL

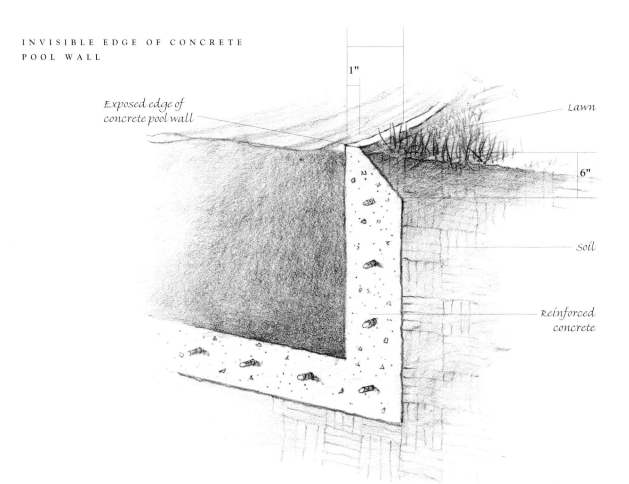

Exposed edge of
concrete pool wall

1"

Lawn

6"

Soil

Reinforced
concrete

OPPOSITE TOP: Boulders placed at the edge and within the shell of the lily pool add a sense of permanence to the Robinson Garden on page 48. The large basin behind the stone planter wall is for marginals, and the concrete divider creates two containers for invasive plants such as Nelumbo spp. and Typha angustifolia.

OPPOSITE BOTTOM: The illusion of water being retained by a stone wall at the John and Susan Ulfelder Garden was achieved by building the wall inside the concrete shell of the lily pool. The shell acts as a waterproof liner.

I like to use an "invisible edge" for certain concrete pools in which the top beam of the pool wall is tapered down at a 45-degree angle away from the water, leaving about an inch of wall thickness visible at ground level at the water's edge (see detail, above). This narrow band is even more inconspicuous when painted black. The "invisible edge" allows you to plant against it right up to the waterline (see the Littlefield Garden on page 140). Lawn also can be brought up to the water's edge in a clean, sharp line (see the Jacobs Garden on page 38). The same effect is possible with a liner by cutting and lifting the sod along the edge and slipping the liner underneath. Use gutter spikes at one-foot intervals to secure the edge.

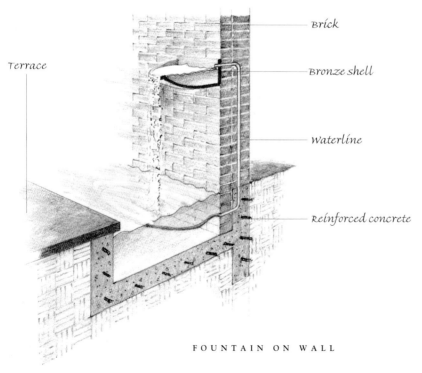

Brick

Bronze shell

Terrace

Waterline

Reinforced concrete

FOUNTAIN ON WALL

ABOVE: A "floating" stone is a convenient way to step across the water. The stone is shaped to resemble a lily pad and set on a hidden concrete pedestal.

LEFT: In the Bennett/Born Garden, water is pumped from the lily pool through a waterline embedded in the brick wall to a sculptural bronze shell, where it overflows back into the pool.

Equipment

Pools and ponds often function best with the help of several pieces of equipment such as a fountain pump, a filter for cleaning the water, an automatic refill valve, a pool de-icer, and lighting. Not all of this equipment is necessary. The equipment you choose will depend on your budget, the amount of automation you desire, and the amount of time you want to spend on routine maintenance.

All of the equipment is electrically operated. To protect against shock, it must be connected to a ground-fault circuit interrupter, or GFI. This is an extremely sensitive device that is used in place of a regular electrical outlet; it shuts off power when it senses a moisture leakage into the outlet or an electrical surge. A licensed electrician should be available from the beginning of your project to install all electrical equipment in the correct sequence. Each stage of the electrical work may have to be approved by an inspector from your local building office.

I always use a submergible pump, which can simply be dropped into the water and plugged into an outlet in the garden (see illustration below). It is inexpensive, and

SUBMERGIBLE PUMP

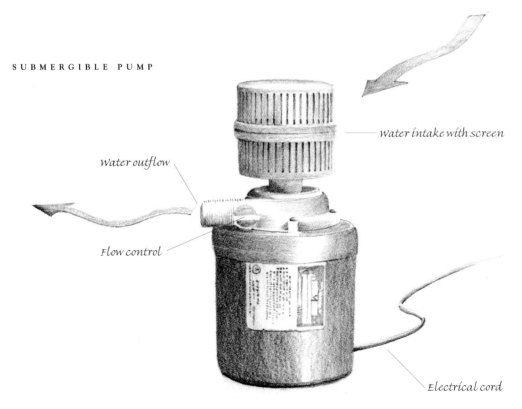

water intake with screen

water outflow

Flow control

Electrical cord

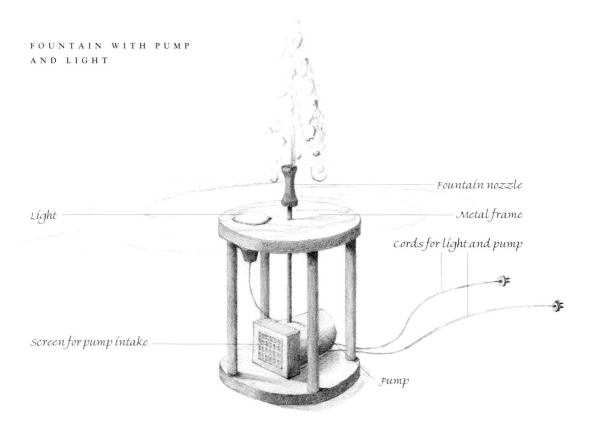

Fountain nozzle

Light

Metal frame

Cords for light and pump

Screen for pump intake

Pump

because it is underwater it is noiseless. I follow several guidelines when installing a pump to circulate water through a fountain, waterfall, or filter. The volume of water circulated through a fountain depends on the design and effect I want to accomplish. To run a mechanical filter, I recommend that the volume of water be recirculated every two hours. With a biological filter, water should be recirculated every four to six hours. To play it safe, I buy a pump that is more powerful than I anticipate I will need, because it is always possible to install a valve to restrict the flow. I place such a valve close to the edge so I can reach it easily.

Fountains are very easy to install. They are sold as prefabricated stands that include the pump, filter, jet, and light (see illustration, above). I set the stand on the floor of the pool and plug its cord into one of the sockets in a separate double outlet in the garden, which is connected to a switch in the house. Using another cord, I plug the light into the other socket in the double outlet connected to another switch in the house.

The fountain nozzle is interchangeable, depending on the kind of jet I choose. This could be anything from a spray to a very thin eight-foot-high column of water. It is also possible to divert the water through an ornament or sculpture placed on land at the pool edge, on top of the wall, or over the water on a concrete block or stone base.

A waterfall is also easy to create by placing the pump in the lowest of several pools

and pumping the water through a hose up to the top pool, from which it falls back into the lowest pool (see the Littlefield Garden on page 140). I use the same pump I would choose for a fountain and control the flow with a water valve.

When I design a fountain or waterfall, I keep in mind that water plants prefer quiet water. Turbulent water can upset the balance of the pool. It is possible to use a baffle to slow down water movement, as I did at Hudson River Park (see detail, page 63).

Filters are optional for a lily pool. A film of algae and sediment will often form on the bottom and sides. Water quality will temporarily diminish with disturbances such as a heavy rainfall. A filter will speedily clarify the water. If a pool contains the correct proportion of fish, snails, and plants, a filter is not necessary (see Part V, "Care," page 195).

I use two types of filters, mechanical and biological. The mechanical filter is the most common. It is a sponge set in a box before the pump's intake (see illustration, page 164, top). A mechanical filter can be placed inside or outside the pool, but a biological filter is always outside the pool. It grows bacteria in layers of gravel, which consume nitrogen and in turn purify the water (see illustration, p. 164, bottom).

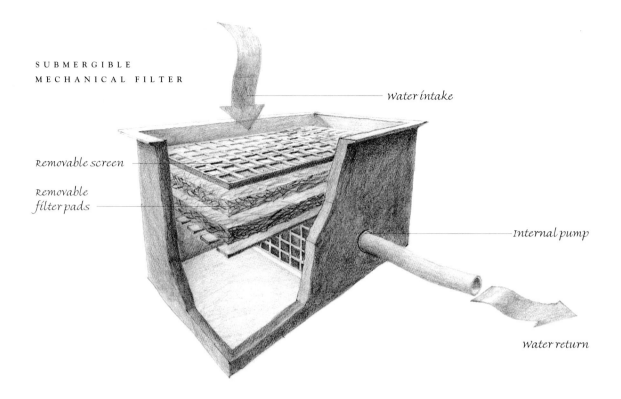

SUBMERGIBLE
MECHANICAL FILTER

Water intake

Removable screen

Removable
filter pads

Internal pump

Water return

BIOLOGICAL FILTER

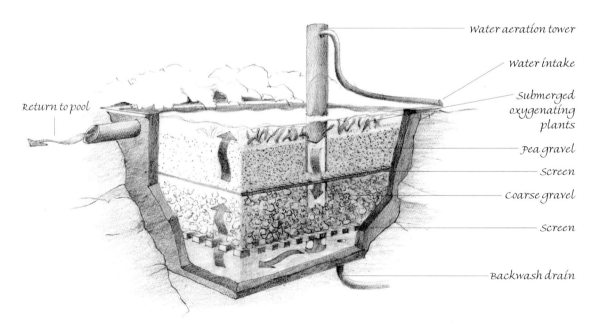

Water aeration tower

Water intake

Submerged
oxygenating
plants

Return to pool

Pea gravel

Screen

Coarse gravel

Screen

Backwash drain

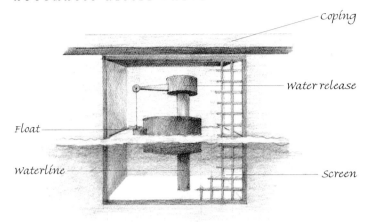

coping

water release

Float

waterline

Screen

In the heat of summer, evaporation causes considerable water loss. To eliminate the need to refill the pool by hose or spigot, I often install an automatic refill valve (see illustration, left). This convenient device uses a floating balloon to automatically maintain a constant water level in the pool.

The automatic pool de-icer is a very inexpensive, thermostatically controlled heating element. In zones one through seven, a de-icer is necessary for pools to keep an area thawed on the surface so fish can survive through the winter. It was developed for farmers to keep their cows' drinking troughs from freezing. I simply drop it in the pool in the fall and plug it into a nearby outlet in the garden that is wired to remain hot. It maintains an ice-free area at least two feet in diameter (see illustration, below).

Finally, I think that lighting is a must for all water features. It extends the interior of the house outside, adds hours to the view, and beautifully reflects plants and trees at the water's edge. I prefer using aboveground fixtures because they are the most flexible. I simply plug them into an outlet in the garden and direct them to special features, such as a waterfall or night-blooming water lilies. The fixture is on a stake pushed into the ground. Prefabricated fountains come with a built-in light for illuminating the water jet or bubble at its base. The light fixture is underwater.

AUTOMATIC POOL DE-ICER

Electric cord

Float

Heating coil

Fish guard

PART IV

PLANT

Roy Lichtenstein, Water Lilies with Willows.
© *Roy Lichtenstein*.

ISSUES

The magic of aquatic plants lies in their beauty and diversity. When I design a water garden I use my knowledge of the growth characteristics and cultural requirements of each plant to achieve a biologically balanced pool.

When it comes to choosing plants for your garden, the aesthetic considerations are almost unlimited. Leaves may be waxy, smooth, ribbed, hairy, or glossy. They may be shades of green, brown, purple or yellow, mottled or variegated. Many plants, such as *Thalia* spp., *Zizania* spp., and *Aponogeton* spp., persist into fall or winter. The hues of their foliage and flowers gradually change as night temperatures drop. The leaves of aquatic and bog perennials often are dramatically shaped.

A plant's flowering characteristics are very important. Consider the colors you want to live with in your garden. A plant's blooming season may occur at any time of the year. I take into account when the garden most likely will be used. A flower's fragrance or foliage also may determine its location.

I apply the same principles in designing a perennial garden to poolside gardens and lily pools. A plant's shape and size and its relation to the garden and surrounding landscape are extremely important. It's also important to vary plant heights. For example, the flat leaves of lilies floating on the water's surface and the lotuses' slightly raised heads draw attention to the pool's horizontal plane. I like to juxtapose vertical varieties, such as *Scirpus* spp. and *Typha* spp.

I also consider a plant's root growth and seeding characteristics. I plant aggressively rooting plants together and let them battle it out for territory. Delicate, less aggressive plant materials should be separated from other plants or planted in containers.

You can determine the number of plants to include in your pool by the kinds of plants you choose, their rate of growth, and the amount of time you are willing to spend keeping the more aggressive species within bounds. I suggest that approximately one third to two thirds of the water's surface be shaded during the hot summer months. This will control algae bloom, keep water temperatures down, and your fish healthy.

The plants you choose depend on your taste and schedule. But keep an open mind; it's fun to experiment with new varieties and to trade root cuttings or tubers with friends who also have water gardens. A pool, like any living organism, constantly changes and evolves. It will not look the same from season to season or year to year. After all, change is one of a garden's great pleasures.

PLANTS, FISH, AND OTHER WILDLIFE

Plants

Selecting the appropriate aquatic plant materials for your pool will ensure that your water garden is a success. This glossary lists a few of my favorite aquatic, bog, and poolside plants that are particularly tough and versatile, and have spectacular and consistent seasonal effects.

The glossary relies on our own experiences in different climate zones and situations. When discrepancies in botanical or common names arose, I turned to *Hortus Third*, a plant dictionary, to settle the issue.

Each listing consists of a description with an accompanying photograph or sketch accentuating the plant's form, flower, or most notable characteristics. I divided the plants into four categories:

Marginals: These are edge plants that thrive with zero to twelve inches of water over the crown of the root system. Marginals prefer moist to wet soils or the shallow edges of the pool. These plants typically create the transition between land and water.

Bog Perennials/Moisture-Tolerant Plants: These plants prefer soils in which the root crown is at or slightly above the water level. Bog perennials do not like to be completely submerged for long periods of time (particularly during the colder winter months). They are common to moist meadows and swales at lower elevations.

Submerged (Oxygenating) Plants: Submerged plants grow on the bottom of the pool in one to four feet of water. These plants are typically grassy aquatic plants that cleanse the water by removing mineral salts and other impurities. These plants outcompete algae for nutrients and increase the available oxygen supply to fish.

Floating-Leaf Aquatics: Lilies, lotus, and nonoxygenating plants fall under this group. Floating leaf aquatics usually have roots at a depth of one to three feet below the water's surface.

Each plant description is listed under its most widely accepted botanical name and spelling. The plant description generally includes its common name, native origin, size, color, shape, flower, blooming period, seeding characteristics, rate of growth, leaf characteristics, seasonal interest, cultural requirements regarding sun or shade, and pH (acidity). I include blooming dates by season rather than month, since this book is intended for worldwide distribution, including the southern hemisphere. Each description also includes notable characteristics regarding growth, care, historical significance or uses, toxicity, susceptibility to pests, and other information that may interest the water gardener. Each plant description is followed by a reference line that provides the following information:

(Z) Zone: The plant hardiness zone map, put out by the United States Department of Agriculture (USDA), delineates the average climatic zones, from warmest to coldest, where the plant has been known to survive successfully.

(H) Height: The average height that each plant can be expected to achieve under normal growing conditions. Height is generally given in a range.

(WD) Water Depth: The average depth of water coverage over the root crown for floating, submerged, or marginal plant material. In situations where plant materials survive in moist or saturated soils but do not survive if submerged completely—e.g., bog perennials—the soil-moisture tolerances are summarized.

Aquatic plants add enormously to the life and beauty of your pool. Their presence will attract many species of wildlife to your garden, such as insects, birds, and amphibians.

But there are also practical reasons for introducing aquatic plants to your pool. They shade the surface of the water to reduce algae bloom; stabilize pond banks, pool bottoms, and shorelines; and provide nesting habitats for waterfowl. Marginal plants help to camouflage our less than perfect attempts to re-create nature by obscuring the sharp edges of concrete pools or fiberglass tubs. Submerged aquatics oxygenate the water and provide spawning protection and food for fish.

Marginals

ACORUS CALAMUS

Sweet flag (*above*) is prized for its upright, slender, irislike foliage, which grows from thirty inches to six feet in height. A native of most regions in the northern hemisphere, its aromatic, citrus-scented root stalks and foliage were used in ancient times for food, medicines, and perfume. The flowers are an insignificant yellow-green, which occasionally develop berrylike red fruit. This slow-growing plant prefers full sun but will tolerate partial shade.
Z: 4–10. H: 2.5–6 feet. WD: 3–5 inches of water cover.

ACORUS CALAMUS 'VARIEGATUS'

Variegated sweet flag shares many of the attributes of com-mon sweet flag. Its compact height of twenty-four to thirty inches and slow growth make it more suitable for smaller water gardens. The foliage coloration is more intense, with distinct green, cream, and rose variega-tions. The flowers are insignifi-cant brownish-green spikes. The plant prefers full sun but will also tolerate partial shade.
Z: 4–10. H: 24–30 inches. WD: 0–5 inches of water.

CALLA PALUSTRIS

Bog arum, or hardy *calla,* inhab-its the rich organic soils of bogs and shallow waters of North America, northern Asia, and Europe. Strong, vigorous roots trail over the water's edge as it multiplies; but it will not grow in flowing water. Glossy, green, heart-shaped foliage dis-plays small, clear-white, lilylike flowers with orange centers. Bright-red fruit often persist into late winter. The bog arum

prefers full sun for best flowering and should not be confused with *Zantedeschia*, the tropical *Calla* lily.

Z: 6. H: 9–12 inches. WD: 0–4 inches of water; propagate by root cuttings taken in spring.

CALTHA PALUSTRIS

The marsh marigold (*opposite*) is a prolific bloomer in Europe, Asia, and North America as far north as Alaska. The abundant display of bright yellow, waxy buttercup flowers occurs in mid to late spring on branching stalks of glossy green foliage. The marsh marigold does well in partial to full shade.

Other notable varieties include: *Caltha palustris* 'Alba', which has white flowers with gold centers, and *Caltha palustris* 'Flore Pleno', the heavy-blooming, double-flowering variety.

Z: 5–9. H: 8–24 inches. WD: 0–9 inches of water.

DULCHIUM ARUNDINACEUM

Dwarf water bamboo (*above*) is an interesting screening or specimen water plant with upright green foliage. This plant is not a true bamboo, as its name implies. It prefers full sun to partial shade and boggy, saturated soils.

Z: 6–10. H: 18 inches. WD: 0–4 inches of water cover.

EQUISETUM HYEMALE

A native of North America, Europe, and Asia, the horsetail rush, or scouring rush (*right*), is a descendant of the giant *Equisetums,* which were abundant throughout the world in geological times. Its high silica content makes its stems useful for scouring and polishing. The horsetail rush has distinctive tubular green stems with dark bands at the joints. Instead of flowering, horsetails, like the fern family, produce spores. Horsetails are vigorous growers and will spread quickly in damp soils if root growth is unrestricted. They prefer full sun to partial shade and create interesting vertical accents in the water garden.

Z: 3–9. H: 3–5 feet. WD: 0–6 inches of water. Gradually increase water depth as plant matures.

GUNNERA SPP.

Known as giant rhubarb (*above*), this enormous plant was discovered in the swamps of southern Brazil and Colombia. Large, deeply-lobed palmate leaves develop in clumps up to ten feet high and eight feet wide. The leaves have thick stalks with prominent prickly vines on the undersides. *Gunnera* produces an unusual, large, rusty-red bottle-brushlike flower in midsummer. Because of its size it should be used sparingly—for example, as a specimen on the edge of large ponds. It is not a plant for confined spaces. *Gunnera chilensis/tinctoria* is a slightly smaller variety that grows in more compact clumps. The flowers and fruit of this species develop deeper shades of red than *G. maniculata*. *Gunnera* prefers full sun but will tolerate partial sun. It needs sun protection in hot climates. In winter, bend over the old and loose leaves to cover the berry crowns for frost protection.
Z: 7–9 with winter protection. H: 6–10 feet. WD: Boggy soils.

HOUTTUYNIA CORDATA

Houttuynia (*below*) is a colorful creeping ground cover for moist areas. It is a native of southern Japan and the mountains of Java and Nepal. Its small, heart-

shaped maroon, blue-green, purple, and cream-colored leaves create an interesting carpet to highlight the more upright foliage of irises and rushes. *Houttuynia* is very vigorous and should be planted in controlled situations. In full sun the foliage displays deeper colors and the white flowers are more prolific. Z: 5–9. H: 6–12 inches. WD: 0. Moist soils only.

IRIS KAEMPFERI

The Japanese iris (*below*), often referred to as the *Clematis*-flowering iris, has beautiful horizontal flower heads in a range of

blue, purple, pink, white, or veined combinations of colors. The leaves are green and sword-shaped with a distinctive mid-rib. This is another boggy-soil plant whose crown should be planted at least two inches above water level. The roots will tolerate up to two inches below water level in the summer; however, the plants may develop root rot if they are too wet during the winter months. Japanese irises require full to partial sun, adequate moisture, and acid soils for best results. Z: 2–8. H: 2.5–3 feet. WD: Moist soils only, or submerged to a 2-inch depth in summer.

IRIS PSEUDACORUS

Yellow iris (*below*) is a native of western Europe and North Africa and has become naturalized throughout eastern North America. Named for its similar appearance to *Acorus calamus*, *Iris pseudacorus* has blue-green, sword-shaped leaves that grow

as high as four feet. It is prized for its profuse early-summer bloom of bright yellow flowers with a slightly orange throat and brown to purple veins. *Iris pseudacorus* prefers full sun and slightly acid soils for best bloom.
Z: 4–9. H: 3–4 feet. WD: 0–6 inches; will tolerate up to 10 inches.

IRIS SIBIRICA

The Siberian iris is a native of central Europe and Russia. The slender two- to four-foot tall foliage displays graceful flowers in blue, white, purple, and wine. Siberian irises prefer rich, damp soil and full sun. Once established, they tolerate drought and partial shade. They are relatively free of insect and disease problems.
Z: 3–8. H: 2–4 feet. WD: Moist soils.

LYSICHITON AMERICANUM

Skunk cabbage (*below*), a member of the *Arum* family, is a native of the northwestern United States. This plant requires rich, water-saturated soils. Large yellow flowers up to twelve inches long emerge early in the spring before the foliage. The foliage may reach a height of up to three feet; the malodorous leaves are best enjoyed from a distance. *Lysichiton* grows well in sun to partial shade with ample moisture.
Z: 6. H: 2–3 feet. WD: 0–3 inches.

MENYANTHES TRIFOLIATA

Bog bean (*above*) is a native of wetlands throughout the temperate northern hemisphere. The bog bean roots at the water's edge and increases by creeping rhizomes, which spread across the surface. Fragrant, delicate, white-fringed flowers with a pink tint bloom in late April through September. Alternate, leathery, olive-green elliptical leaves occur in clusters of three. The plant has vigorous but controllable growth, which can be cut back easily and rooted from the cuttings. Bog bean prefers full sun but tolerates partial shade and neutral to acid soil.
Z: 2–9. H: 6–9 inches. WD: 3–5 inches.

ORONTIUM AQUATICUM

Golden club (*opposite top*) is an interesting specimen for the water garden. This native of the southeastern United States is prized for its unusual slender white flower spikes tipped with yellow, which bloom from mid-spring to summer. The leaves are from twelve to eighteen inches in length, silvery blue-

KEN DRUSE PHOTOGRAPH

EILEEN EMMET PHOTOGRAPH

green, and elliptical. They float on the water's surface or are held erect just slightly above. The blue-green berries are inconspicuous. The plant prefers full sun but tolerates partial shade.

Z: 6–10. H: Floating leaves can be held 12 inches above water surface. WD: 3–12 inches. Does best if started in shallow water, gradually increasing depth. Will tolerate depths up to 18 inches.

PISTIA STRATIOTES

Water lettuce (*above*), a tender floating aquatic native to South America, has downy soft gray-

green leaves resembling a miniature lettuce. Its long white feathery roots gradually turn black as they mature, providing a good spawning cover for fish and amphibians. The graceful rosette of leaves held just above the water's surface protects small, insignificant flowers, which later develop into young seedlings. It is not hardy. Z: 8. H: 5 inches. WD: Floating.

PONTEDERIA CORDATA

Pickerel weed (*below*) is a native of both North America and South America. It has broad, glossy, heart-shaped to sword-shaped leaves with rich violet-blue flower spikes held high above dense foliage clumps. Its flowers provide a brilliant display from summer to autumn,

and it is a strong but not rampant grower. Dark purple and white varieties are available. The plant prefers full sun and roots in marsh banks and shallow waters.

Z: 3–10. H: 2.5–3.5 feet. WD: Wet soil to 6 inches water cover.

P. lanceolata is a similar species but is not as hardy. Z: 7–10. *P. azurea* is a taller species. Z: 5–9. H: 3–4 feet.

SAGITTARIA SPP.

Sometimes referred to as arrowhead, the swamp potato, or duck potato, is an interesting plant recognized by its arrowhead-shaped leaves. It is a vigorous grower, but its tubers are also food sources for waterfowl, which may make it difficult to establish in certain areas.

SAGITTARIA JAPONICA 'FLORE PLENO'

The double-flowering arrowhead is a native of Asia. *Sagittaria japonica* 'Flore Pleno' grows much slower than the native American species and the double-white flower heads are larger and rounder. This plant is widely cultivated in the rice paddies of Asia for food. *S. japonica* (up to thirty inches tall) is taller than *S. japonica* 'Flore Pleno' and has dark red leaf stems and single white flowers. Z: 7–10. H: 12–24 inches. WD: 0–6 inches.

SAGITTARIA LATIFOLIA

A native of North America, this variety of arrowhead has light-green arrowhead-shaped foliage with a three-petaled white flower that blooms in late summer. The root tubers were once an important food source for the Native Americans. Arrowhead prefers full sun to partial shade and mucky, acid soils. Z: 5–10. H: 24–36 inches. WD: 0–12 inches.

SAGITTARIA RIGIDA

Sagittaria rigida (*above center*) is a native of North America. The deepwater duck potato has light-green foliage in mixed lance-

shaped and arrowhead-shaped form. The plant prefers full sun but will tolerate partial shade. Z: 6–10. H: 24–30 inches. WD: 0–30 inches.

SAURURUS CERNUUS

Lizard's tail, also known as water dragon or swamp lily, is an interesting perennial herb, native to eastern North America. Its nodding white flower spikes are four to twelve inches long and pleasingly fragrant. The pointed, tall, heart-shaped leaves provide good fall color late in the season. Lizard's tail prefers full sun to partial shade. Z: 4–9. H: 3–5 feet. WD: Plant in 0–6 inches of water.

SCIRPUS LACUSTRIS TABERNAEMONTANI 'ALBESCENS'

The white bulrush (*right*) is common to Europe and has tall,

slender, cylindrical, rushlike stems. Its creamy-white foliage is marked horizontally with pale-green bands. It has a vigorous root system that should be contained and prefers full sun but will tolerate partial shade. Z: 5–10. H: 3–5 feet. WD: 3–5 inches of water cover.

THALIA DEALBATA

The hardy water *Canna* (*see page 172*) is a native of semitropical and tropical regions of the United States. Its broad-leaved, blue-green *Canna*-like foliage is followed by interesting loose reddish-purple flower panicles on dramatic stalks that grow up to ten feet. The plant prefers full to partial sun and requires some

ful, light-green, reedlike leaves with dense brown flower spikes that bloom in midsummer. The plant prefers full to partial sun and will root on the banks of marshes and in shallow waters. Its aggressive rootstalks may become invasive if planted in wetland areas and should be planted in a tub or container in a pool situation. It also will seed itself in favorable conditions. Other notable varieties include *T. latifolia,* which is good for large-scale naturalizing and shore stabilization, and *T. shuttleworthii, T. minima,* and *T. laxmannii,* all of which are slender-leaved dwarf varieties that grow as tall as two to three feet and are ideal for small pool situations, but more difficult to obtain. Z: 3–10. H: 6 feet. WD: 0–12 inches.

protection in winter. Other notable varieties include the red-stemmed *Thalia geniculata rubra,* which is not hardy. Z: 6–10. H: 6–10 feet or more. WD: 0–12 inches. May grow out of water in a marsh situation. It needs the protection of water above the root system to prevent frost damage.

TYPHA ANGUSTIFOLIA

The narrow-leaved cattail (*above*) is a native of North America, Europe, and Asia, and has grace-

ZIZANIA LATIFOLIA

Wild rice (*below*), a native of eastern Asia, is an ornamental marsh grass that is cultivated for food and woven mats, and is used in lily pools for its broad, ornamental, grasslike foliage and long flower panicles. Wild rice prefers full sun and shallow, muddy, marshlike conditions. The flower panicles may grow as long as two feet with silvery purple individual grains up to three inches long. It is a very aggressive plant and will need restriction. It will seed itself in favorable locations. Z: 7–9. H: 3 feet. WD: 3 inches to 3 feet.

Bog Perennials/ Moisture-Tolerant Plants

ASCLEPIAS INCARNATA

Swamp milkweed (*above*) inhabits wet, boggy meadows in North America, from Nova Scotia to Florida. Fragrant, quarter-inch-wide rose-pink to purple flowers are displayed in grouped umbels at the ends of densely branched plants. Slender, pale-green lancelike leaves three to six inches long grow in groups of two or three along the stems. The seedpods are two to three and a half inches long and produce silky white hairs that are airborne once the seeds mature. Swamp milkweed prefers full sun and damp soils for best flowering. Other notable milkweeds include *Asclepias tuberosa,* the orange-flowered butterfly milkweed, which prefers sandy, well-drained, average-to-poor soils but does not tolerate saturated soils, and A. *syriaca,* common milkweed, a native American plant with green to purple flower umbels. The seeds and roots are prolific in wet soils and may prove too invasive for general use.
Z: 3–9. H: 4–5 feet. Soil: Moist.

ASTER MACROPHYLLUS

Bigleaf aster (*right*), a native of North America from Quebec to Tennessee and naturalized in Europe, is a useful woodland perennial that tolerates wet soils. Bigleaf aster has large, heart-shaped leaves and clusters of one-inch pale-lavender-fading-to-white daisylike flowers with yellow centers that bloom in midsummer. Bigleaf aster prefers full sun to partial shade and moist-to-average soil conditions, but it also does well under trees competing with tree roots. *Aster macrophyllus albus* has white flowers.
Z: 3–8. H: 3–4 feet. Soil: Moist to average.

BACCHARIS HALIMIFOLIA

Groundsel, or sea myrtle (*opposite top*), is a useful shrublike plant for coastal gardens because of its resistance to salt spray and saline soils. A native of the

dunes, salt marshes, and tidal riverbanks of eastern and south coastal United States, this plant also adapts to seasonal dry-soil conditions. Sea myrtle has separate-sexed plants that produce beautiful brilliant white flower heads in late summer and fall. The female plant also produces showy thistlelike heads of white fruit after flowering. The leaves are coarsely toothed, two and a half inches long, and gray-green in color. This adaptable, fast-growing shrub prefers full sun and moist soils for best flowering and can tolerate heavy pruning to control its height.
Z: 5–9. H: Up to 1 2 feet. Soil: Moist; will tolerate dry soils once established.

CAREX SPP.

The genus *Carex* comprises nearly two thousand species of grasslike perennials related to the sedge family. *Carex* are common throughout the world, particularly in temperate and Arctic regions. Most *Carex* inhabit wet or moist soils and are at home when planted near water. *Carex* help naturalize and blend other showier perennials and marginals. Many *Carex* are evergreen or semievergreen and can extend the seasonal interest of the garden with their foliage and typical brownish flowers. The following *Carex* species are just a few of many commercially available varieties currently available.

CAREX ELATA 'BOWLES GOLDEN'

Golden tufted sedge is interesting when planted at the water's edge or in masses. The golden leaves with green margins reflect on the dark still waters of the pool. *Carex elata* is native to Europe and Scandinavia.
Z: 5–9. H: 2–3 feet. Soil: Wet to moist.

CAREX MUSKINGUMENSIS

Palm sedge (*below*) is a native of western North America and has many pale-green grasslike leaves that grow in crowded tufts resembling palm fronds. Palm sedge creates a good backdrop for more colorful or vertical marginal accent plants near the pool's edge. It prefers partial shade and moist soils.
Z: 5–9. H: 2 feet. Soil: Moist.

CAREX PENDULA

Drooping sedge (*below top*) is commonly found in wet clayey soils in shady woodlands and near water. The large semievergreen leaves are broad and pendulous. The late-spring inflorescence are interesting brown, drooping catkinlike flowers. A native of Europe, Asia, and North Africa, the drooping sedge prefers full to partial shade and cool, moist soils, but it will tolerate sunnier conditions, provided ample moisture is available. Drooping sedge can be planted in masses or used as a vertical accent among other sedge species.
Z: 5–9. H: 24–36 inches. Soil: Wet or moist; clayey.

CHELONE LYONII

Pink turtlehead (*bottom*), a native of North America, is an interesting bog perennial for sunny wet meadows and shady streamside plantings. The rose-pink flowerhead resembles a tortoise head and is as showy as a snapdragon when in bloom. It prefers full sun and moist, organic rich soils but also tolerates partial sun and clay soils. The serrated, glossy green leaves die back to the ground in winter. This plant must have adequate moisture but, once established, will seed freely and bloom for long periods in late summer.
Z: 5–8. H: 24 inches. Soil: Moist.

DARMERA PELTATA

Umbrella plant (*below*), formerly termed *Saxifraga peltata* or *Peltiphyllum peltatum*, is a native bog plant from Oregon and the northern mountains of California. It is named for its

umbrellalike, large, round-toothed leaves, which can reach up to twenty-four inches in diameter and are held by three-foot-long petioles. *Peltiphyllum* has a more compact and refined form than *Petasites* (*see page* 186). The bronze-green foliage takes on an intense, russet-red hue in autumn. Umbrella plants prefer moist, shaded locations. A dwarf form includes *Darmera peltata* 'nana', which grows twelve to fifteen inches high and six to nine inches wide. Z: 5–8. H: 24 inches. Soil: Wet to average.

EUPATORIUM PURPUREUM*

Joe-Pye weed (*below*), a native of eastern North America, is a tall showy bog or meadow plant with large flowers of fuzzy purplish clusters that attract butterflies. The leathery leaves occur

in whorls of three to five inches along the purplish stems. Joe-Pye weed prefers full sun to partial shade and moist conditions; once established, it is fairly drought-resistant. Flowering time is midsummer. *Eupatorium purpureum x* 'Gateway' is a more compact form.
*syn. *E. fistulosum*
Z: 4–9. H: 5–6 feet. Soil: Moist to average.

EUPHORBIA PALUSTRIS

Wood spurge (*above*), a native of Europe and southern Asia, is a versatile perennial for woodlands and bog gardens. It has showy yellow-green flower heads that bloom in early spring and narrow, elliptical apple-green leaves on slender woody stalks. *Euphorbia* does well in full sun and in moist-to-wet soils, but once established it will tolerate some shade and drier conditions. All *Euphorbias* have a white sap that is poisonous and irritates the skin upon contact. It will seed itself under favorable conditions.
Z: 4–8. H: 3–6 feet. Soil: Wet to average.

HELIANTHUS ANGUSTIFOLIUS

The swamp sunflower (*page* 184, *top*) inhabits the bogs and swamps of North America from New York to Florida. Showers of three-inch-wide daisylike yellow flowers with purple-brown centers adorn the tall narrow grasslike leaves in October. Swamp sunflowers prefer full sun and moist soils.

Overfertilization may make the plant floppy and require staking. *Helianthus salicifolius* looks similar, but will not do well in wet conditions and needs very good drainage.

Z: 6–9. H: 5–7 feet. Soil: Moist.

HIBISCUS MOSCHEUTOS

Rose mallow (*below*), a spectacular native bog plant from the salt marshes of the eastern coastal United States, is valued for its huge hollyhocklike flowers of pure white, pink, rose, crimson, or bicolors. The hollow canelike stalks may achieve a height of up to six feet, with brilliant late-summer flowers from four to nine inches in diameter. Rose mallow prefers marshy to moist soils in full sun but will tolerate average soils and partial shade, as long as the roots are kept moist. Rose mallow often is planted toward the rear of perennial borders, at the pond edge, or as a backdrop in natu-

ralized marsh conditions. The dried stems and seed heads often persist late into the season and provide winter interest.

Z: 5–9. H: 4–6 feet. Soil: Moist to marshy; salt tolerant.

KOSTELETZKYA VIRGINICA

The native seashore mallow (*below*) shares the same brackish

coastal marsh environments (from New York to Florida) as its close relative, the rose mallow. Small in form and flower, the two- to three-inch-wide flowers are pale pink and bloom in mid to late summer. Seashore mallows prefer full sun and moist-to-wet soils, but they can tolerate drier, sandier soils than the rose mallow.

Z: 5–9. H: 3–4.5 feet. Soil: Wet to average.

CAROLINE SEGUI-KOSAR PHOTOGRAPH

LOBELIA CARDINALIS

Red cardinal flower (*above*) occurs in the shady swamps and marshes of North America from New Brunswick to Florida. Sparks of vivid scarlet flowers adorn the purple-bronze upright stems in late summer. Attractive rosette-shaped lancelike leaves add interest. Cardinal flowers prefer wet soils and shaded locations. A layer of mulch for winter protection may help ensure survival in colder climates. The plants tend to die out after flowering. Seedlings will appear in favorable locations.
Z: 2–9. H: 2–4 feet. Soil: Moist to wet.

LOBELIA SIPHILITICA

Blue cardinal flower, another North American native that occurs from Maine to North Carolina, has beautiful long-lasting lavender-blue flowers on slender flower spikes in late summer. The lancelike light-green leaves are irregularly toothed at the margins. Blue cardinal flowers prefer full to partial shade and moist, organic soils; they also tolerate slightly drier conditions than the red cardinal flower. At one time this plant was believed to cure syphilis—hence the name—but like most cardinal flowers, it may be poisonous if ingested.
Z: 5–9. H: 2–3 feet. Soil: Moist to wet.

LYSIMACHIA CLETHROIDES

White gooseneck, or loosestrife (*below*), is a native of China and Japan. This vigorous bog perennial has a strong root system that may overwhelm a small garden with moist soils. The flowers are long white curving spikes that resemble a goose's neck. The glossy green leaves turn bright red in late fall. This plant prefers full sun to partial shade and moist soils. Its vigorous root system is good for slope stabilization. To prevent it from invading other plants, surround *Lysimachia* with growing plants such as *Hemerocallis* and *Pennisetum*. The roots of *Lysimachia* cannot penetrate these areas.
Z: 4–9. H: 2.5–3 feet. Soil: Moist to average.

ONOCLEA SENSIBILIS

Sensitive fern (*above*) is widely distributed in shady marshes and bogs throughout North America, Europe, and eastern Asia. The pale-green, deeply lobed fronds are bronze-red when they emerge in early spring. The dense root systems are prolific in wet, acid soils. Sensitive fern is also a good edging plant for pools. Its vigorous roots will actually grow into the water. The fern derives its name from its sensitivity to early frosts and its tendency to curl up at the edges if the fronds are picked. In early fall the majority of sterile fronds die back at the first frost; the black sporing fronds persist late into the winter, adding seasonal interest. Sensitive fern prefers sheltered, shaded locations and moist soils.

Z: 4–9. H: 18–36 inches. Soil: Moist.

PANICUM VIRGATUM

Switch grass (*see photograph, page 24*), a native grass of Central and North America, produces airy, billowy sprays of seed heads on stems three to eight feet tall. Planted in masses, these grasses produce beautiful textures from spring through fall. In early fall the pale-green grasses and seeds turn yellow, and certain varieties then turn to red, plum, or russet-brown in late fall. These plants prefer full sun and moist meadowlike situations but withstand considerable dryness after the plant has established itself. It will seed itself under favorable conditions.

Notable varieties include:

P.V. 'Haense Herms': Red-plum fall color.

P.V. 'Heavy Metal': Erect metallic blue, turning yellow in fall.

P.V. 'Rotstrahlbusch': Vivid red fall color.

Z: 5–9. H: 3–8 feet, depending on variety. Soil: Moist.

PETASITES JAPONICUS

Japanese butterbur (*below*) is a native of Japan,

Korea, and China. It is noted for its huge cabbagelike leaves, which are more than eighteen inches wide and three or more feet tall. Its large leaves were used to wrap blocks of butter, hence the name butterbur. It is a harbinger of spring with early-blooming, whitish-purple panicled flower heads on long spikes. This plant is a deep-rooted, prolific grower for trouble spots where other plants refuse to grow. Its tenacious growth can also be its most troublesome attribute, making it difficult to control or eradicate once it is established. Used sparingly, Japanese butterbur can deliver striking effects near the water's edge. The variety 'giganteus' may grow six feet tall, with leaves three to four feet in diameter. *Petasites* is cultivated in the Orient for its edible leaf stalks. It prefers full sun to partial shade and plenty of moisture.

Z: 4–9. H: 4 feet or more. Soil: Wet to average.

STACHYS PALUSTRIS

A native of Europe, marsh betony is a fast-growing and covering marsh plant that prefers moist conditions. It has small, oblong leaves and pinkish-purple spike flowers that bloom from June through September.

Z: 5–9. H: 3 feet or more above water surface. WD: 6 inches.

VERNONIA NOVEBORACENSIS

New York ironweed (*below*) is native to bogs and wet meadows from Massachusetts to Georgia. Ironweed is an ideal plant for naturalizing with other moist meadow perennials. It is prized for its loose clusters of dark-purple, daisylike flowers, which bloom in late August through October. The foliage is narrow, lancelike, and slightly pubescent below. It prefers full sun, is tolerant of many soil conditions, and transplants quite easily. Ironweed is good for late-season color accents to complement the rich autumn hues of wetland grasses and sedges.

Z: 5–9. H: 3–6 feet. Soil: Moist to average.

Submerged (Oxygenating) Aquatic Plants

ALISMA SUBCORDATUM

Water plantain (*above*) is a marginal aquatic, native to ponds, streams, and marshes in the eastern United States. It grows on the surface of the water or in wet ground beside the pool or pond. In June or July the plant is covered with pyramidal panicles of inconspicuous flowers with petals that are white to rose-pink. The flower stalks become woody after flowering and make excellent dried flower arrangements. Spent flower heads should be removed if seeding becomes a problem. Water plantain prefers full sun to partial shade.
Z: 5–10. H: 2–3 feet. WD: 2–6 inches.

ELODEA CANADENSIS

Pondweed (*below*), a native of temperate North America, is now naturalized throughout much of Europe. This submerged oxygenating aquatic herb has delicate whorls of green fernlike foliage in groups of three on long, slender dark-green stems. Pondweed grows just below the water's surface

and is often used in home aquariums because of its good spawning cover and excellent oxygenating characteristics. Rampant growth may occur if the plant is left unchecked, but this can easily be controlled by planting in containers where growth can be removed or reduced.

Z: 6–10. H: Remains below the water's surface; stems grow from 1–3 inches long. WD: Floating, 0–12 inches.

MYRIOPHYLLUM AQUATICUM

Parrot's feather (*below*) is an important oxygenating plant with whorls of delicate, finely cut, feathery green foliage that creeps along the water's surface. A native of Brazil, Argentina, and Chile, it has been naturalized in the southeastern United States. The foliage provides protection and spawning areas for fish and amphibians. Male and female flowers are borne on separate plants in the axils of submerged leaves, and therefore are not visible. Foliage tips take on a crimson-bronze hue in late summer and early fall. The plant prefers full sun and tropical conditions. Plant along the water's edge so that stems can trail over the surface, on the pond's bottom, or in a container. It is hardy in northern climates if planted below freezing levels.

Z: 6–10. H: 6–9 inches above water level. WD: 3–12 inches.

RANUNCULUS AQUATILIS

Water crowsfoot, a submerged oxygenating aquatic native of Europe and North America, has small white buttercup flowers with gold centers that bloom in midsummer. Beautiful kidney-shaped leaves float on or below the surface, providing texture to the water garden. Crowsfoot thrives in sunny wet meadows and marshes, or in pools of water with up to twelve inches of water coverage.

Z: 5. H: 24 inches. WD: 0–12 inches.

Floating Leaf Aquatics (Lilies, Lotus, and Nonoxygenating)

APONOGETON DISTACHYUS

The water hawthorn (*above*) is a floating aquatic, native to South Africa, with interesting straplike green foliage blotched with purple. Its white flowers with black anthers are fragrant and showy. It blooms in early spring or late fall, often persisting through midwinter in temperate zones. It is an interesting plant for the early and late season, when other plants are not showy. It prefers sun but tolerates partial shade. The seeds are water-dispersed, floating then gradually sinking to the bottom, where they germinate in shallow areas.

Z: 3–10. H: Floating leaves; flowers 2–4 inches above water surface. WD: Plant in 0–6 inches of water; transplant as needed as deep as 30 inches of water.

HYDROCHARIS MORSUS-RANAE

Frog's bit, a diminutive floating plant native to Europe and Asia, has fine, silklike roots and miniature one-inch-wide lilylike pale-green leaves. The small white flowers with yellow centers bloom throughout the summer. Flower buds fall off in the fall and plants sink to the bottom of the pool, where they remain dormant until spring and emerge as new plants. Frog's bit is hardy in pools where the wintering buds are below the freeze line. The plant prefers alkaline conditions and full sun. Unfortunately, the lush green mats of foliage are susceptible to snail damage. Z: 5–9. H: 0–2 inches above water surface. WD: 0–6 inches.

MARSILEA DRUMMONDII

Water clover (*below*), or common nardoo, is a tender aquatic that grows in floating, submerged, or marginal situations. This plant originates in Australia and is a member of the fern family.

Water clover is grown for its four-lobed, cloverlike leaves with small white hairs. It prefers full sun to partial shade. Water clover is a strong growing plant and may have to be reduced periodically. Z: 6–10. H: Up to 12 inches. WD: 0–6 inches.

Plants benefit from applications of aquatic fertilizers every two to three weeks and can survive the winter if the rootstalk is well below ice level. Notable varieties include: *N. lutea*, or native American lotus, including cultivars 'Momo botan' (double pink flower with yellow center), 'Chawan basu' (white flower with pink edges), and 'Mrs. Perry D. Slocum' (double pink flower fading to yellow).
Z: 4–10. H: 3 feet or more above water surface. WD: 1–3 feet.

NUPHAR LUTEUM

Hardy water lilies belong to two categories, *Nymphaea* and *Nuphar*. *Nuphar* prefer more acidic, deepwater conditions than *Nymphaea*; they do not flower as freely and therefore are usually chosen for conditions in which *Nymphaea* will not survive as well.

Nuphar luteum, or pond lily, which is similar to *Nymphaea*, has heart-shaped floating leaves and yellow buttercuplike flowers in midsummer. Its creeping rootstock grows in a water depth of six feet or more. This plant is tolerant of substantial shade and some running water.
Z: 3–10. H: 1 foot or more above water surface. WD: 6 feet or more of water cover.

NELUMBO SPP.

The lotus (*above*) is a showy, interesting aquatic with large, bluish-green leaves up to three feet wide above the water's surface. Its large, peonylike flowers grow in many colors, and its prized flower seedpods resemble the funnel of a watering can and are often used in dried flower arrangements. Rootstalks are very aggressive and should be planted in a container or planter to prevent them from overcrowding other aquatics. Lotus prefers a warm location in full sun with little wind. It will tolerate some shade and cooler water, but will flower less profusely under these conditions.

NYMPHAEA X HYBRIDA

There are many varieties of water lilies both hardy and tropical blooming. The bloom may range in color from pure white to pink, yellow, blue, red, and lavender. Some are day-blooming and night-blooming and have fragrant flowers. Leaves may be green or mottled, large or small. Choices are virtually unlimited and are dependent on the color scheme of the garden. *Nymphaea* have a rootstock that can grow up to six feet in water depth, depending on the variety. Dwarf cultivars grow best in shallow water of six to twelve inches. Water lilies prefer calm water and at least six hours of sunlight. In fishponds, *Nymphaea* are best planted in containers in clayey soil. Every two to three years water lilies should be divided and transplanted to prevent overcrowding. Tropical blooming *Nymphaea* can be grown in the summer in colder areas but do not survive the winter outdoors. New plants should be used every summer season.

Z: 3–10. H: 1 foot or more above water surface. Leaves float above water; flowers held slightly above water surface. WD: 6 feet or more of water cover.

NYMPHOIDES PELTATA

A native of Europe, *Nymphoides* (*above*) features small floating leaves and looks somewhat like a miniature version of *Nymphaea*, with yellow flowers in summer. This plant prefers warm conditions, full sun, and a water depth of at least four inches. It spreads rapidly and aggressively but can be controlled easily by raking or hand-pulling rhizomes.

Z: 5–9. H: Leaves float above water; flowers held slightly above water surface. WD: 4 inches to 2 feet.

Fish and Other Wildlife

Fish add life, color, and motion to a pool, and are an important element for maintaining a biologically balanced pool. Not only are they fun to watch and feed, but they also control algae, plant growth, and insects, such as mosquitoes.

You should not introduce fish to the pool until five to six weeks after construction. By that time the water pH should be stabilized around 7 to 8. To determine the correct number of fish for your pool, determine the number of gallons that your pool contains and figure approximately one inch of fish for every three to five gallons of water. It is better to start out with fewer fish and add more if desired than to overpopulate the pool.

You will undoubtedly transport fish to your pool from the aquatic nursery in a plastic container or bag. Acclimatize new fish to the pool by floating the container or bag in the pool for fifteen to twenty minutes so it can reach the same temperature as the water in the pool. When the temperatures are the same the fish can be released into the pool. Most fish can survive under temperatures ranging from extreme cold to warm; however, sudden temperature fluctuations can shock and injure fish.

Make sure that the pool habitat is suitable for fish. Shade from mid- and late-afternoon sun should be provided by vegetation and floating, leaved plants. Protection such as overhanging stones and submerged pipes allow fish to hide from larger fish, birds, or raccoons. Water plants also require protection from fish and benefit from a two- to three-inch layer of pea gravel, which keeps fish from fanning mud and dislodging the roots of aquatic plants with their tails. Plants provide spawning areas, protection from sun and predators, food, and oxygen.

A large lily pool in Japan is designed with a deep rectangular place where fish can find cooler water and protection from predators.

There are many types of fish in all shapes and colors to choose from. The common goldfish comes in orange, black or white, or mixed colors. Common scaled varieties include the comet-tail, Japanese fantail, and the black Chinese moor. Scaleless or transparent-scaled goldfish such as shubunkins and calico fantails come in a wider spectrum of colors, including blues and lavenders that are highly prized in Japan.

Fish are as different as people and no two are exactly alike. Golden and silver orfes are sleek surface-swimmers and like to leap through fountain sprays and moving water. Their quick flash of color can be fun to watch. They travel in schools. Carp and koi are much more docile pets. Higoi (usually pink or orange metallic color) and nishiki koi may reach a size of three to four feet or more in length and may live as long as seventy years.

Bottom feeders and scavenging fish, such as the green tench, are helpful in removing debris from the pool floor but are not necessary for balancing a pool. Some bottom feeders may be aggressive and may attack other fish. Snails such as the ramshorn snail, recognizable by their flattened shell, which they carry upright on their back, are desirable additions to the pool community because they help control filamentous algae. Other snails are considered pests and may eat water-lily leaves and the shoots of emergent plants.

Frogs, turtles, salamanders, and other types of amphibians and wildlife will migrate to this new oasis in your landscape. Birds will drink and splash in the pool. Fish will leap at trespassing insects. All types of life will prosper in your new pool.

PART V

CARE

~~~

Pool maintenance varies and is subject to many considerations. Shape, size, depth, and geographical location influence the amount of effort that is necessary to create a biologically balanced environment.

Large pools are generally easier to maintain. The bigger and deeper the pool, the less fluctuation there is in temperature. If the temperature of your pool changes, the water may cloud and algae is more likely to bloom.

You should site the pool to avoid potential problems that increase maintenance. The pool should have positive drainage away from its edges. A lily pool is not a device to cure storm water-drainage problems. Runoff into a pool may contain contaminants such as soluble salts and fertilizers, or inorganic substances that will affect the water's quality and may even kill plants and fish. Organic matter, leaves, and soil washoff may increase algae activity in the pool, making it difficult to have clear water.

Most aquatic plants prefer full sun and shelter from wind. Too much sun will encourage algae to bloom; too little could make your flowering plants become spindly and weak. If your pool is close to trees, you may face a very troublesome maintenance problem. In autumn, falling leaves will sink to the bottom and begin to decompose. Tannins leach from the leaves into the water and deplete the water's oxygen. When possible, you should remove debris from the pool's surface before it sinks to the bottom.

Attempting to control the pool's chemistry only temporarily solves the potential problems associated with pool maintenance. Algaecides are a quick but temporary cure for problems that could be solved permanently by introducing floating-leaf or oxygenating plants, or by correcting problems of drainage or water circulation. Successful water gardens are the result of proper planning and are maintained by achieving a biological balance.

The following is a description of routine pool maintenance, by the season:

SPRING: At the beginning of the gardening year, cut and remove dead foliage and shoots before plants start to grow. Heavy feeders, such as *Nymphaea* spp. and *Nelumbo* spp., should be fertilized, replanted, and divided. Pump filters and lines should be cleaned. At midseason, tropical floating-leaf aquatics, such as *Eichhornia crassipes,* should be placed on the water surface to reduce sunlight in the pool. Due to winter rain and snow, leaching of a concrete pool shell might make the water more alkaline or acidic; adjust the pH as necessary.

SUMMER: This is the season to relax and enjoy the lush beauty of your pool. Watch for water evaporation and top off the pool with a hose if you do not have an automatic refill valve.

FALL: Before the leaves begin to fall, stretch a net across the pool to collect them. This is especially important if the pool is near a woodland. Fall is the time to remove tuber plants for storage before the weather gets too cold. These plants should be stored in a cool, dry place. The pool should be cleaned by temporarily dropping the water level by one-half to two-thirds in order to easily shovel the year's deposits of leaves, organic matter, and fish waste onto adjacent garden planting beds.

WINTER: Finally, to end the maintenance year, float your automatic pool de-icer on the water and turn off all pumps and fountains. If the pool freezes over, do not crack the ice with sudden blows. I know of cases where playful children have broken the ice and killed fish by the resulting shock waves. In shallow, unheated pools that are north of Zone 5, you may want to move fish indoors for the winter.

PART V
RULES and REGULATIONS

The first thing to know about rules and regulations is that each local jurisdiction has its own guidelines, usually written in the local zoning and building codes. These codes define the type of pool or pond that is under consideration and list specific regulations concerning location, permits, and construction.

When pools have electrical wiring in or next to a pool, the local electrical codes must be consulted for the location and installation of such devices. These regulations will define the minimum distance for siting electrical outlets from the pool edge for all of your pumps, junction boxes, and lighting connections.

When construction, planting, or grading is to occur in areas designated as wetlands and/or waterways (streams, ponds, creeks, etc.), permits may be necessary at local, state, and federal levels. The U.S. Army Corps of Engineers usually is the federal agency responsible for administrating and enforcing the provisions of Section 404 of the federal Clean Water Act. You are encouraged to contact your local office for permit guidance prior to starting project plans or construction.

In many jurisdictions the national codes of the Building Officials and Code Administrators International (BOCA) constitute the basis of the rules and regulations. It is very important that this document be referred to early in the decision-making process.

BOCA defines pools for swimming or bathing as those that are greater than 24 inches deep with a surface area greater than 250 square feet or a pool that is equipped with a water-recirculating system or involving structural materials. BOCA also provides regulations regarding the location on the property, the structural design of wall and floor slopes, surface cleaning devices, steps and ladders, water supply, treatment and drainage system, and pool-area enclosures (fences and walls). In most situations, lily pools and swimming pools have specific regulations governing the height of the pool fence enclosure and the hardware for the gate(s) that must be self-latching and self-locking. The BOCA national codes are designed for adoption by state and local governments by reference only. Jurisdictions adopting BOCA may make necessary additions, deletions, and amendments in their interpretation of the code.

SELECTED REFERENCES

Allison, James. *Water in the Garden*. Morris Plains, N.J.: Salamander Books, Ltd., 1991.

Axelrod, Dr. Herbert R., Albert Spalding Benoist, and Dennis Kelsey-Wood. *Garden Ponds*. Neptune City, N.J.: T.F.H. Publications, Inc., 1992.

Brookes, John. *Gardens of Paradise*. New York: New Amsterdam Books, 1987.

Church, Thomas D., Grace Hall, and Michael Laurie. *Gardens Are for People*. New York: McGraw-Hill Book Company, 1983.

Eliovson, Sima. *The Gardens of Roberto Burle Marx*. Portland, Ore.: Sagapress/Timber Press, 1991.

Hendel, Hubert, and Peter KeBeler. *Wasser im Garten*. Niedernhausen/Ts., Germany: Falken Verlag GmbH, 1988.

Heritage, Bill. *Ponds and Water Gardens*. London: Blandford Press, Ltd., 1992.

Higuchi, Shoichiro. *Water as Environmental Art*. Tokyo: Kashiwashobo Publishing Co., Ltd., 1991.

Hortus Third. Revised and expanded by the Staff of the Liberty Hyde Bailey Hortorium. New York: Macmillan Publishing Company, 1976.

Itoh, Teiji. *The Gardens of Japan*. Tokyo: Kodansha International, 1984.

Kaufmann, Edgar, Jr. *Falling Water, a Frank Lloyd Wright Country House*. New York: Abbeville Press Publishers, 1986.

Ledbetter, Gordon. *Water Gardens*. New York: W.W. Norton & Company, Inc., 1980.

Mills, Dick. *Garden Ponds*. Morris Plains, N.J.: Salamander Books, Ltd., 1992.

Mosser, Monique, and George Teyssot. *The Architecture of Western Gardens*. Cambridge, Mass.: MIT Press, 1991.

Motta, Flávio. *Roberto Burle Marx ea nova visão da paisagem*. São Paulo, Brazil: Livaria Nobel S.A., 1984.

Oehme, Wolfgang, James van Sweden, and Susan Rademacher Frey. *Bold Romantic Gardens*. Reston, Va.: Acropolis Books, Ltd., 1990.

Paul, Anthony, and Yvonne Rees. *The Water Garden*. Ontario, Canada: Viking Penquin, Inc., 1986.

Perry, Frances. *Waterlilies and Other Aquatic Plants*. New York: Henry Holt & Company, 1989.

Plumptre, George. *The Water Garden*. London: Thames & Hudson, Ltd., 1993.

Robinson, Peter. *Pool and Water Gardening*. Portland, Ore.: Timber Press, Inc., 1988.

Russell, Stanley. *Water Gardens*. North Pomfret, Vt.: David & Charles, Inc., 1985.

Stein, Siegfried. *Wassergärten*. Munich: BLV Verlagsgesellschaft mbH, 1989.

Swindells, Philip, and David Mason. *The Complete Book of the Water Garden*. Woodstock, N.Y.: Overlook Press, 1990.

Swindells, Philip. *At the Water's Edge*. London: Ward Lock, Ltd, 1991.

Swindells, Philip. *The Overlook Water Gardens Handbook*. Woodstock, N.Y.: Overlook Press, 1984.

The New Royal Horticultural Society Dictionary of Gardening. Vols. 1–4. Edited by Anthony Huxley. New York: Stockton Press, 1992.

Thomas, Charles B. *Water Gardens for Plants and Fish*. Neptune City, N.J.: T.F.H. Publications, Inc., 1988.

Water Gardening. Vol. 41, No. 1, Handbook #106. Edited by Janet Marinelli. Brooklyn, N.Y.: Brooklyn Botanic Garden, Inc., 1990.

Wienke, Karl. *Mein Wassergärten*. Leipzig: Neumann Verlag, 1990.

Wieser, K. H., and Dr. P. V. Loiselle. *Your Garden Pond*. Melle, Germany: Tetra-Press, 1992.

OPPOSITE: *After being pumped to the top black granite tray, water rains down in musical splashes from tray to tray into the lily pool.* JOHN NEUBAUER PHOTOGRAPH

CREDITS

Photographers

JAMES VAN SWEDEN
unless otherwise noted

———

Design Participants with van Sweden and Oehme

CASCADE AND ESPLANADE IN MANAHATTAN
Carr, Lynch, Hack & Sandell, architects

THE DAVID E. RUST GARDEN
Hugh Newell Jacobsen, architect
Lester Collins, landscape architect

AN ELLIPTICAL POOL IN A TOWN SETTING
Wiebenson & McInturff, architects

THE GERMAN-AMERICAN FRIENDSHIP GARDEN
Leo A Daly, engineers

PARADISE MANOR
Sorg Associates, architects

THE PAUL L. HOUTS, JAN MUNHALL-HOUTS GARDEN
Hugh Newell Jacobsen, architect
Lester Collins, landscape architect

ROCK RIM PONDS
Divney Consulting, engineering and planning

STILL POND
Dean Design Incorporated, architects

TWIN BRIDGES
Muse-Wiedemann, architects

WATERFALL AND POOL IN THE CAPITAL CITY
M. Paul Friedberg, landscape architect

OPPOSITE: *The underwater planter, shown here on the far side of the lily pool in autumn, is lush with* Typha angustifolia, Nelumbo lutea, *and* Scirpus tabernaemontani *'Albescens'.*

INDEX

ABOUT THE TYPE

THIS BOOK WAS SET IN GOUDY VILLAGE NUMBER 2, A TYPE-
FACE DESIGNED BY FREDERIC WILLIAM GOUDY (1865-1947).
GOUDY BEGAN HIS CAREER AS A BOOKKEEPER, BUT DEVOTED
THE REST OF HIS LIFE TO THE PURSUIT OF "RECOGNIZED
QUALITY" IN A PRINTING TYPE. GOUDY VILLAGE NUMBER 2
WAS PRODUCED IN 1932, AND ALTHOUGH IT IS BASED ON THE
TYPES OF JENSEN IT BEARS A RESEMBLANCE TO THE FAMOUS
GOUDY OLD STYLE.